D1553273

JOURNAL I, 1945–1955

MIRCEA ELIADE

JOURNAL I
1945–1955

Translated from the Romanian by Mac Linscott Ricketts

THE UNIVERSITY OF CHICAGO PRESS

Chicago and London

This book was originally published in France by Editions Gallimard, Paris, as pp. 1–228 of *Fragments d'un journal I*. © 1973 by Editions Gallimard.

The University of Chicago Press, Chicago 60637
The University of Chicago Press, Ltd., London
© 1990 by The University of Chicago
All rights reserved. Published 1990
Printed in the United States of America

99 98 97 96 95 94 93 92 91 90 54321

Library of Congress Cataloging-in-Publication Data
Eliade, Mircea, 1907–
  Journal.
  Vols. 1 and 4 translated from the Romanian by Mac
Linscott Ricketts; V. 3 translated from the French by
Teresa Lavender Fagan.
  Reprint (v. 2) Originally published: No souvenirs.
New York : Harper & Row, 1977.
  Contents: 1. 1945–1955 — 2. 1957–1969 — 3. 1970–
1978 — 4. 1979–1985.
  1. Eliade, Mircea, 1907–   . 2. Religion historians
—United States—Biography. I. Title.
BL43.E4A3313 1989   291′.092 [B]   89–36220
ISBN 0-226-20416-2 (v. 1 : cloth)

Contents

Translator's Preface

This volume of Mircea Eliade's journal, although numbered "I," is in fact the fourth to appear in English translation, due to editorial exigencies. Like volume IV for 1979–85, this volume, Eliade's "Parisian Journal," is translated directly from the Romanian in which it was written, rather than from the French as were volumes II and III.

Though entitled "Volume I," this book is by no means the first portion of Eliade's private diary to have been written. Eliade began keeping a journal in the spring of 1920 at age thirteen when he was a student in the third year of lycée in Bucharest. Soon he was maintaining in notebooks several kinds of journals simultaneously: on his voluminous readings, scientific observations and experiments, boy scout adventures, the conversations and activities of his friends, and personal thoughts and feelings. These diaries became the raw material for some of the articles, sketches, and short stories he began to publish in juvenile periodicals in late 1921. By the time he was eighteen, he could count a hundred articles from his pen that had appeared in print—a goodly number of them derived directly or indirectly from his journals. He even wrote a lengthy "novel" of his adolescence, *The Novel of the Nearsighted Adolescent*, consisting in large part of verbatim dialogues and anecdotes first recorded in his copious notebooks of the lycée years.* A sequel, *Gaudeamus*, covering a part of his university years and his first romance, likewise was written autobiographically, but only part of it was drawn from the journal, the remainder being invented. Miraculously, many of the original manuscripts from these early years have survived: after being discovered in the eighties, some of them have been published in Romania. It is sometimes possible to trace the evolution of a chapter of *The Novel of the Nearsighted Adolescent* from a notebook-journal to its final form.

When he returned to Romania from three years of study and adventure in India in December 1931, Eliade brought with him a suitcase "overflowing with notebooks and folders" (as he recalled in his preface to *No Souvenirs*, his journal for 1957–69). From these notebooks consisting of personal diaries, travel notes and observations, and philosophical reflections, he would publish a number of books, including *Santier* (called a novel, but frankly acknowledged to be an annotated selection of entries from his Indian diary), *Soliloquii* (a book of philosophical musings and fragments taken from another journal—as proved by a surviving original manuscript recently found and published), *India* (from travel diaries), and the prize-winning novel *Maitreyi*, in which the line between diary and fiction is impossible even today to draw.

Eliade continued to keep a diary throughout the thirties, but except for the travel journal he wrote in the summer of 1937[†] and possibly a few other fragments—unidentified as such—published as articles, all these invaluable records seem to have been lost during the war years. Eliade left all his papers and books behind when he entered diplomatic service abroad in 1940, and he was unable to retrieve them later.

As a cultural attaché, Eliade served first in England (April 1940 to January 1941) and then in Lisbon (until the end of the war). It is highly

---

*See my account of Eliade's early life in *Mircea Eliade: The Romanian Roots, 1907–1945* (Boulder: East European Monographs, 1988). Eliade's novel, *Romanul adolescentului miop*, was published in 1989 in Bucharest, edited by Mircea Handoca.

†Published in English as an appendix to Chapter 15 of Eliade's *Autobiography II* (Chicago: University of Chicago Press, 1988). Eliade was very proud of this summer's journal.

probable that a journal beginning in January 1941 exists among Eliade's papers in Chicago; his autobiography from this point onward appears to draw from such a written source. A few fragments from this "Lusitanian Journal" have been published in Romanian emigré periodicals, and a short excerpt is included in the English translation of Eliade's *Autobiography II* at the end of Chapter 18.

The entire manuscript of Eliade's journal is said to contain more than five thousand notebook pages. It is deposited in the Special Collections division of the Regenstein Library of the University of Chicago. For the present, in accordance with the author's wishes, it is sealed, although eventually it will be made available to those who desire to read it, both in America and in Romania. (Two photocopies exist, as well as the original.) When Eliade published the first selections from his journal in English he stated that the parts he had released for 1945–69 represented less than one-third of the full journal text for those years. Having been given a photocopy "sample" of some of the pages for one of those years, I can attest that much, indeed, has been omitted in the published selections, and also that some rephrasing has been done to improve the literary quality of the parts made public.

There is no question that Eliade accorded much importance to his journal. He was, from youth, an avid reader and critic of other persons' journals. His comments on various journal writers and their works can be found throughout this and other volumes of his journal. Journals were, perhaps, his favorite form of reading matter. Once in Paris, when funds for food and rent were low, he could not resist buying a well-known author's journal which he saw displayed in a bookstore window. Later he regretted doing so, because the book disappointed him: the writer, he says, didn't have the "knack" for writing a private diary (22 September 1946). And yet he believed that "a journal is always interesting, because it is a 'document' and at the same time a *témoignage*" (4 October 1945). Eliade's preference was for "journals that abound in ordinary notations, remarks about visits, routine happenings, dreams, illusions—signs that the author wrote the journal for himself" (5 October 1945). It was such a journal that Eliade himself strove to write, and one that would save, "by 'freezing' them, fragments of *concrete time*'' (15 December 1946) so that the experiences and feelings he had known then could be *relived* by him, rereading the journal in future times. As he wrote on 8 February 1953:

> I write in order to be able to reread later. I don't care whether someone else reads me later, but I don't write for him. I write to find myself again later, to remind myself of times uselessly lost (*all* "times" are irreparably condemned, however much we may endeavor to save them).

His journal, then, was Eliade's first line of defense against his great enemy Time, his most effective weapon for resisting its destructive power. Or, put otherwise, it was his sacred history, his personal mythology—to be reread and relived. Yet it was also for him a literary genre which he, as a writer, was striving always to perfect, having, I believe, one eye on that future reader and cherishing the hope that perhaps through the journal, if not through his "scientific" and literary works alone, he would obtain immortality. It is for this reason that I look forward with much anticipation to the day when the complete text of Mircea Eliade's journal will be disclosed to the public and we can read the candid record of his remarkable life as he recorded it.

Even so, as it is, a wide window has been thrown open through the pages of the journal which Eliade chose to make available to us. The years covered in this book, 1945–55, were very difficult and even crucial ones for the author. Recently widowed and jobless, cast into exile in a foreign land at age thirty-eight and forced to live by writing in an alien tongue, Eliade wrestles with poverty and its humiliations, despair over his homeland, and uncertainty about the direction he should take professionally as he looks toward the future. Harassed and slandered by enemies from Romania, he finds attractive prospects evaporating like mirages. Publishers make promises and then postpone publication, debts mount, and he suffers attacks of "vagotonia." But there are points of light too, as learned savants at the Sorbonne and other universities discover Eliade's writings and praise his scholarship and insights. Gradually, in 1950, the tide turns: he is invited to participate in Eranos conferences; he lectures at Paris, Rome, and elsewhere; he participates in the International Congress on the History of Religions; he learns he will receive a monthly stipend from the Bollingen Foundation. In that year too, he remarries. From this point on, the progress is steady, though each step upward is won only at the cost of tremendous effort.

To a large extent, this volume is the journal of the writing of *Noaptea de Sânziene* (called in English *The Forbidden Forest*), Eliade's only postwar novel and undoubtedly his supreme literary achievement. The redaction of the novel was protracted over some five years, 1949–54, and it was accompanied by innumerable distractions, interruptions, and setbacks. While Eliade has narrated the story of his writing of the novel in *Autobiography II* (Chapter 22), one begins to understand what the effort cost him only by reading the journal for these years. In this English version of the journal excerpts I have been able to restore to the text a number of passages pertaining to the novel's composition that were cut from the French version, presumably because of space limitations. Thus the reader of this volume will be able, for the first time, to trace the growth of the book in all the agonizing detail Eliade originally intended to share. This portion of the journal, appropriately, reaches its climax on the day the novel reaches *its* climax, 26 June 1954. The handful of entries that follow seem like a dénouement to the story. Perhaps significantly, Eliade ceased writing in his journal for two years soon after that, just as the novel was about to be published in French.

For a more connected and balanced account of Eliade's life during these years, the author has given us his *Autobiography*. Although the latter was written with the journal in hand, each book contains much of importance not found in the other. (For example, one finds few references here to Christinel, whom Eliade married in 1950—see the abrupt and matter-of-fact notation of that event in the entry for 9 January 1950—but a whole, beautiful chapter is devoted to her in the *Autobiography*.) But for a sense of the day-to-day life of the man, for a candid insight into his thoughts and feelings, the journal is the place to look. Those who have known Eliade only through his "works of erudition" and admired him for his scholarship, need also to come to know him as a man through his journals and autobiography, and as an author through his novels and shorter works of fiction.

These notes are being written some two months after the overthrow of Ceauşescu and of the Communist regime that began in Romania at the end of the Second World War. How many times have I thought as I have rejoiced in these sudden developments: if only Mircea Eliade could have lived to see this day! As this journal portion and others of his writings make plain, Eliade deeply loved his native country and never ceased to long for it—though forced to live away from it for more than half his life. Some of the most poignant passages in this volume are those in which Eliade expresses his difficulty in accepting his status as a permanent exile, resigning himself to the probability that he would never see his homeland again (cf. 22 November 1951, for example). Regrettably, the liberation came four years too late for Eliade to be able to enjoy it. But there is some consolation in the knowledge that, from now on, anything and everything he wrote will be allowed to circulate freely in the land of his birth.

The ultimate responsibility for this translation is of course my own, but I wish to thank Christinel Eliade for her invaluable assistance.

Mac Linscott Ricketts
Louisburg College

17 September 1945

We arrived yesterday morning, Sunday, 16 September. Cioran had reserved two rooms for us at the Hôtel de l'Avenir, 65 rue Madame. This morning I went to the legation. Long discussion with Bianu—memories of the winter of 1940–41 at Oxford and London.

Routine matters: registration at the police station and the court house, food ration cards, etc.

18 September

What a strange feeling, to imagine myself writing in another language! I'll have to begin to write in French before I know it well. But the thing that bothers me most is, I don't know at all the public I'll be addressing. Supposing I'll have a few readers: who *are* they?

How may courageous things I allowed myself to try in Romanian—just because I knew my readers!

19 September

For the first time at the Louvre. Venus de Milo, seen at my age, thirty-eight, does not thrill me. And yet I can't decide to walk away; it's as though I were still waiting for her to "reveal secrets" to me. Her head, which at first I didn't like, begins to fascinate me. That look which passes above our heads does not proceed from human eyes, and it is inadequate for perceiving objects in the world of ceaseless becoming; it perceives only ideal, archetypal forms. Hence that strange expression of ironic bliss which the image of the goddess reveals after a few minutes of concentrated contemplation. The same expression is also on the faces of Indian divinities and on those of ascetics in deep meditation. Comparable to the expression on human faces in erotic or mystical ecstasy or in a "trance" of the yogic type. The eyes are excessively sunken, almost disappearing into their sockets. Certain corpses provoke the same phenomenon. The emergence from the world of forms and becoming annuls the eyes. Any ecstasy tends to abolish sight. Ecstasy—the instantaneous penetration into the universe of ideas, of perfect, divine forms.

I must write down in full all that Cioran told me about the woman who, during the Occupation, carried on a black market in coffins.

26 September

Since arriving, I haven't read a single newspaper. I'm trying to detach myself completely from events and concentrate exclusively on my work. When I run out of money, I'll see what I can do. Until then, I'm a writer, orientalist, and historian of religions, forced to live the life of a student—but not absolutely that of an émigré, at least!

27 September

I call on Elencuţa Văcărescu. She says she's just reached eighty-one. And yet, how charming, how poised, how desirous to please, to impress, to overwhelm you! She begins by praising my books about India, although I know very well she hasn't read a single line of them, that she learned about all these things from M. B. She utters a lot of pretentious banalities about music, Latin, religion, and so on. In the first five minutes she told us (I was with Cioran) about her engagement to Prince Ferdinand. The English sovereigns took up her defense, and only this high-placed protection saved her. Because, once he learned of her engagement to Ferdinand, King Carol and all the royal and princely German families isolated her completely, raising around her a wall of deadly silence, etc. For that reason she hates Germans. In France she was able to earn a living thanks to her "oratorical talent." But she has not perverted her pronunciation like so many Romanian women do, who, after a few years in Paris, "make the mouth like a chicken" and cluck the way they think the French women do.

"Quelle destinée!" she exclaimed several times. What kept her alive was her work. In those four years of the Occupation she wrote a great deal—poetry, novellas—and she concluded her memoirs, which can be published in their entirety only after her death.

Wonderful anecdotes about Barrès, Proust, Contessa de Noailles, etc. Probably these topics belong to her program for first meetings with writers.

2 October

I reread *L'Eau et les rêves*. Bachelard speaks very beautifully about "l'imagination de la matière." I should like to show (perhaps in an essay: "L'Eau, les rêves et les symboles") that the imagination constitutes an instrument of cognition, because it reveals to us, in an intelligent and coherent form, the modes of the real. Bachelard believes that a symbol has a psychological history. This may be true; but what interests me is the fact that, once constituted, the symbol is invested with a double function: "existential" and "cognitive." On the one hand, a symbol unifies various sectors of reality (aquatic symbolism, for example, reveals the structural solidarity among Water, Moon, becoming, vegetation, femininity, germs, birth, death, rebirth, etc.). On the other hand, the symbol is always *open,* in the sense that it is capable of revealing "transcendent" meanings which are not "given" (not *evident*) in immediate experience. For example, the rites of baptism reveal a plane of the real other than the biocosmic (birth-death-rebirth): they reveal the "spiritual birth," rebirth to a transcendent mode of being ("salvation," etc.). The aquatic symbol is not only a "fidelity to a fundamentally oneiric temperament" (Bachelard) but also a means of intuiting the real in its totality, because it reveals the fundamental unity of the Cosmos. A symbol becomes autonomous at the moment when it is constituted as such, and its polyvalence helps us to discover homologies among different modes of our being—homologies which the simple "imagination of matter" could not make possible.

4 October

I spend the afternoon with Eugène Ionesco. Long conversation. He tells me he has written several hundred more pages in his journal in recent years, but he wonders, who will be interested in it? In Romania, and everywhere else as well, another generation has arisen. Our generation is finished. . . . I reply that a journal is always interesting, because it is a "document" and at the same time a *témoignage*.

5 October

In the Jardin du Luxembourg, I read *Extraits d'un journal* by Charles du Bos. Sitting on a bench in the sunshine, at a relatively quiet hour, sensing at one and the same time autumn, Paris, and the miracle of existence.

Of course, Charles du Bos's *Journal* is mainly a diary of his work in progress, being a volume rich in quotations, written or dictated in a leisurely manner, and concerned exclusively with books, authors, and "creators." I have the impression that for du Bos life means primarily the possibility of reading, rereading, commenting, and *understanding*. He is, nevertheless, an enthusiastic person. Intelligent things, and said with sensitivity and precision. But I realize that I prefer journals that abound in ordinary notations, remarks about visits, routine happenings, dreams, illusions—signs that the author wrote the journal for himself.

6 October

Commenting on a Gospel verse, "You are all brethren," Charles du Bos observes that Jesus did *not* say: "You are all equal." People are equal only in the sense of "l'égalité des âmes par rapport au salut" [the equality of souls in regard to salvation]. Also this admirable observation: "Ne pourrait-on même soutenir que c'est parce que les hommes sont inéguax qu'ils ont d'autant plus besoin d'être frères?'' [Can't we even maintain that it is because men are unequal that they need so much to be brothers?] (p. 92).

7 October
   This evening, at Vieux Colombier, *Meurtre dans la cathédrale.* Deeply moved in act 2 listening to the chorus lamenting, evoking the nothingness that will swallow the unsaved after the Last Judgment. The void, nothingness, the wheel that keeps turning forever, the seasons that roll on to eternity—I am sure they obsessed T. S. Eliot and terrorized him up to the moment of his conversion. (But only until then? . . .)

8 October
   I begin the writing in French of a little book, *Techniques du Yoga,* based in large measure on my thesis of 1936—which today seems to me unreadable and badly constructed.

9 October
   At Cioran's place I meet a young Frenchman, a survivor of the concentration camp at Buchenwald. Of the many particulars I learned, I note just these two: anyone who had even a single louse went to the disinfecting room and didn't work for a whole day. A day of rest appealed to everyone. And so there came into being a black market in lice. They were sold for a mark apiece—secretly, of course. But the buyer took care to wear the lice somewhere in sight, in order to be sent to the disinfecting chamber.
   In a camp of women of I don't know what locality, a brothel was introduced. Six Frenchmen were selected. The maximum they could have per day were four women. After a month they were returned to Buchenwald, completely drained, and almost all of them died soon afterward.
   Would it ever be possible to make literature out of such happenings in which dementia and bestiality are surpassed only by the grotesque and the absurd?

16 October

They sky is so blue, the parks so melancholic, that I can hardly stay in my room and work!

18 October

The few hours I spend in room no. 18, fourth floor, Hôtel de l'Avenir, I dedicate to the book, *Techniques du Yoga*. I write with considerable difficulty, reproducing whole pages from *Yoga* (1936). I don't want to devote too much time to it; so many other books, half-written or scarcely begun, are waiting—books that seem more important and more on *my own*.

Today at doamna* Rosetti-Roznovanu's place I met Ilarie Voronca, whom I had not seen since 1933. He spoke to me of his tragedy—writing poetry in a language other than his mother tongue. How well I understand! My difficulties in writing essays and scientific prose seem like nothing compared with what he is facing. How on earth does he do it? But it's obvious that Voronca's poetry in the French language is *something other* than what he would have written had he continued to express himself in Romanian.

25 October

Georges Dumézil proposes to me again today that I hold lectures at l'Ecole des hautes études about any subject I wish. Having arrived at Paris too late, I would not be paid for this year; but next year I would be paid for certain, though modestly.

I'm very happy—because it's something I honestly didn't expect and at the same time it's a confirmation that the work I've done so far in my own country is scientifically valid also beyond the borders. But I'm very hesitant too, because I'm afraid of getting myself involved in the erudition and culture of a university, something I believe in less and less.

Doamna is the Romanian equivalent of "Mrs."—TRANS.

1 November

Invited to dinner by Lica C., together with Cioran and Herescu, I meet the director of cinematography and a stage manager, both of whom have had extensive experience in concentration camps and prisons. The stage manager, a Jew, went through Buchenwald and Dachau; when he was released, he weighed only eighty-six pounds. Both said they discovered a new "human condition" in prison: they became convinced that man is *something other* than they had formerly believed; that there is such a thing as spiritual reality, that indescribable "states" do exist. The director of cinematography had wanted to meet me just to tell me this, to find out whether these states that he had experienced had any connection with Yoga.

What a shame that such experiences aren't recorded in private diaries or memoirs, that they are not communicated, discussed, and interpreted! Several millions of Europeans have followed recently an itinerary which society has not known since the Middle Ages. They have been convinced of the reality of "states" they would have smiled about a few years earlier. Skeptics or cowards before being locked up, they led in the camps and prisons a life of sacrifice, they came to believe in a spiritual reality which surpassed them but at the same time consoled them and helped them to survive. Now, as they both admitted, they would faint if someone should fire a revolver suddenly behind their backs. Nothing remains, they said, except the memory of an "absolute" and the certainty of its existence. And all that magnificent experience will be lost, just as I lost all that was revealed to me in Himalaya. Man's capacity to forget is infinite.

3 November

At the conservatory for a concert of old music, "Ars rediviva," arranged by Claude Crussard. Several pieces by Bach, among them the Fugue no. 4 and the symphony for violin and orchestra (unable to recall exactly when I heard it the first time—but I'm sure it was when I was an adolescent: I remembered very well the "adolescent" quality of the emotions). At first hearing, I am astonished at the Concerto in C Flat for violin and orchestra by J. M. Leclair. I didn't even know the name of this French composer whose concerto I do not hesitate to place alongside the best works of Vivaldi.

23 November

Am concentrating, without enthusiasm, on drafting the little book, *Techniques du Yoga*. Many pages are being transcribed from my doctoral thesis, a mediocre work of youth. I believe, nevertheless, that I have succeeded in expressing more clearly my current understanding of the structures and functions of these Indian techniques. Yoga takes its place alongside the many other paradoxical religious attempts to obtain, here on earth, the coincidence of being and non-being, to become "god" while yet remaining man. The paradox of the one "liberated in life" *(jīvan-mukta)*: he has obtained "absolute freedom" and is completely "deconditioned," and yet he continues to live in temporal duration.

24 November

This evening with Ştefan Lupaşcu at the apartment of the young painter Mario Prasinos. He shows us only about seven or eight canvases, among them an admirable Magdalene and an astonishing portrait of a girl. The latter was perhaps the most successful thing I saw in his studio. But all his paintings interested me.

Lupaşcu marvels that I am so taken with a picture in which, he says, I "see" things—symbols not seen by others. I reply that I see such symbols because they *are there*. If another person doesn't see them, it doesn't mean they *don't exist* but simply that he can't see them.

I said further to Lupaşco that my familiarity with the graphic folk creations of Asia and the arts of "primitive" peoples facilitates my understanding of certain contemporary painters. Take that hideous old woman by Prasinos (which no one has liked, owing especially to the green patina on the deep wrinkles that furrow her face): I believe that such a woman *can exist*. I believe in her reality, because I have seen enough African and Melanesian masks in which those who had made them *believed*. True, when a Melanesian or African looks at such a mask, he knows he is seeing a spirit, an ancestor, someone who does not belong to this world, while that woman in the painting is the "mask" of a person still living. But how do we know that Prasinos has not seen just *this kind of death* in the countenance of the woman?—that he has made the mask hideous precisely because it seemed to him that that is the only authentic graphic representation for a being who participates in this world only physically, who in reality is devoid of life and survives only in a carcass?

25 November

Sunday. At 2:00 I go to Louis Renou's place. He, together with Dumézil, will present me to the Société Asiatique. Renou lives on rue Emil Faguet, at Port d'Orléans. A modern building; his apartment on the sixth floor. He himself answers the door: middle aged, with a bright, cordial face, casually dressed (how I admired his shiny pants!), he speaks to me with insight and admiration about my book *Yoga* (1936). In a library-office, with gigantic card files, a fire is burning in a cast-iron stove. A great window takes in the whole sky. Soon Madame Renou appears and serves us coffee, while shortly afterward the door opens and in comes a little child on all fours. "It's the only warm room and we all stay here," Mme. Renou explains.

Sensational news about Dasgupta. (Renou also gives me a long letter of his from Cambridge to read.) Dasgupta has been settled in England for three or four years. He hopes to be offered A. B. Kieth's chair in Sanskrit at Edinburgh. He is awaiting the appearance soon of the fourth volume of *A History of Indian Philosophy*. But—and this is the sensational part—he announces that he has also written (to cite only a few): a history of Sanskrit literature in nine hundred pages; a history of modern Western philosophy in fifteen hundred pages; a history of religions and religious philosophies in fifteen hundred pages; a system of philosophy in fifteen hundred pages; in Bengali, a novel, already published, and four thousand poems, of which only a part have been published, plus a play; etc., etc.! Renou was astounded; I, less surprised. I remember how he worked and how he wrote in 1930.

And, as also in 1930, he is obsessed with ailments. He suffers from heart trouble and many other things, and he wonders whether he will live to see the whole oeuvre in print. Probably all those voluminous works were dictated—as he dictated to me, in the summer of 1930, his book on the Upanishads. Flowing, prolix, with numerous lengthy quotations, the book grew at the rate of thirty pages per day. With one or several English secretaries, Dasgupta's output could break all records!

2 December

I receive a letter from Mrs. Sassoon in which she informs me that all my books left in her care at Oxford in 1941 have been lost! The first of my libraries which I am now *sure* I've lost. Over five hundred volumes—which I shall never again be able to purchase, which I doubt I should ever be able to locate again, because I collected them for the most part from old bookshops in Oxford and London. A simple letter, telling me that this library was lost in the course of four changes of residence. . . .

13 December

I go to the home of Dr. P. L. Couchoud, who had told Dumézil that he wanted to meet me, for the purpose of my possibly contributing to his series, *Mythes et religions.* An old man with a Vandyke, rather portly, likable, sprightly. I heard long ago how Couchoud, when he was a youth, had lost his firm Catholic faith: on a study voyage, stopping too long in Japan, he had hung around the Geishas for several months. He returned from that trip a young and happy skeptic. Since then he is what is an intelligent, often brilliant . . . dilettante.

Listening to him talking about the myth of "the god Christ," I remembered the year 1923–24 when I read his little book which had recently appeared, *Le Mystère de Jésus.* He is truly fascinating. He repeats to me what R. P. Lagrange once told him in Jerusalem: "You and Renan together could present a very correct image of Jesus." Renan historicized Jesus while Couchoud elevated him again very high, situating him among the gods. That is why, he adds, Catholics attack him, but not too vigorously, whereas Protestant and Jewish scholars do not forgive him. Robert Eisler was happy to be able to reconstruct what, in his opinion, represented the *physical portrait* of Jesus. A man, a little man, like Eisler's Jesus—*this* Jewish scholars can accept . . . in order to be able to calmly reject Christianity, the religion created by an ordinary human being. But a god, one who resembles Yahweh, is an inconceivable blasphemy! . . . Thus Couchoud explains the attacks of Jewish scholars. As for the Protestants, they prefer a mere man and a series of "historical facts." To liberal theologians, a god is an affront.

16 December

Reading today, in the bright morning sunlight, a few pages from Henri Michaux, my joy at having discovered a new, great poet was clouded by the thought of my own real, concrete estrangement from literature. It's been three years since I wrote almost anything. I'll wake up some day an old man, with a shelf of learned books beside me: my *oeuvre.* Was this my destiny?

But how can I write anything in a language I don't know well, one that resists me as soon as I try to "imagine," to "dream," to "play" in it?

31 December

I work all day on the manuscript of the French translation of a few chapters of *Prolégomènes à l'histoire des religions.* It's as if I wanted to conclude the year with an especially meaningful effort.

19 January 1946

I have been working almost all the time on correcting the first chapters of *Prolégomènes,* which will constitute also the first lectures at l'Ecole des hautes études. I have given up the idea of writing an inaugural lecture, contenting myself with the few introductory pages of the book, after which I shall enter directly into a presentation of celestial hierophanies.

Brice Parain advises me to redo certain chapters in *Techniques du Yoga* and to add more pages of analysis and commentary, which will permit the Western reader to penetrate not only the universe of Indian thought but also the world of mystical techniques, hopes, and nostalgias.

20 January

Am rereading the books of Schebesta and Trilles about the culture of the Pygmies in the tropical forest. It is amazing how those blessed people *live in the present,* "in the moment." They are incapable of mental concentration, of remembering appointments they have made, or of anticipating the future. The paradisaical phase of humanity. They live as the birds of the air on what the women gather in the forest, on what the men can bring down with their bows. Nomads, they are bound to nothing. They live only in the present, outside "history." Without pursuing any religious objective, they dance day and night. *Homo ludens.* They borrow their drum from their Negro neighbors, to avoid having to carry it with them on their wanderings. Their adornments consist for the most part of leaves. All that is beautiful is temporary, ephemeral. They do not know how to paint, as do the Bushmen. Their camps are undecorated.

21 January

Caught up in a great deal of business, I neglect this journal. And even when I do take the notebook from the drawer, I "consecrate" scarcely two or three minutes to it. My superstitious respect for "useful time," that is, time dedicated to *work* properly speaking: scholarly reading, notes, writing. And out of all this "useful time" methodically consumed, what remains? How many memories, what sort of understandings (I was about to write, "what *revelations*")? . . . Then too, I'm lazy about writing. After so many concerts (in the past week alone I've attended two of Bach), I ought to write a few observations or at least record the programs, for the pleasure of recalling them later. But I must open the drawer, take out the notebook, hunt for my pen. . . .

22 January

The more I learn about the history of religions, the more convinced I become that man is not made for *religion* (in the full and noble sense of the term). The most "primitive" societies, the Australians, Fuegians, and Pygmies, for instance, have known Supreme Beings: all-powerfull, creative, "lofty." But nowhere has the belief borne fruit, nowhere has it transformed man. On the contrary, belief in Supreme Beings is found everywhere in a state of decadence (when it is not completely forgotten), and in the place of honor there appear inferior forms of religious experience: totemism, manaism, animism, etc. "Primitive" man—and civilized man as well—hankers after demonic, orgiastic powers, spectacular divine figures, extravagantly "moving" deities. He does not remember "God" until after he has become convinced that none of these sacred powers can help him. And so, in the archaic worlds also, one arrives at God out of despair. It would be possible to compare Kierkegaard's despair and his taking refuge in the absolute God of Abraham with the despair of the African who, after he has knocked on all the doors of the sacred, turns to the Supreme Being (until then scarcely remembered) as a last resort.

8 February

I began today the course at l'Ecole des hautes études. Other than a few Romanians, only Dumézil and the Tibetanist Marcelle Lalou were present. I read, rather badly, the prepared text (an excerpt from the chapter about the sky god, from *Prolégomènes*). Actually, it is only an academic ritual. I'd have liked for it to have been something else: for example, "play" *(lila),* that is, creative spontaneity, confrontations, dialogue.

1 March

It began snowing yesterday. Today I saw boulevard Saint-Germain covered with snow and students throwing snowballs at one another in front of the Sorbonne. I went inside and gave my lecture. The snow, something I hadn't seen for six years, cast me back in time to my winters in Bucharest. . . .

4 March

I go today to the home of Paul Masson-Oursel, 12 rue de l'Etoile, to meet him at last in person. He is an old gentleman, exceptionally likable, jovial, and lively. I find him dressed in a black shirt and wool trousers. He shakes my hand warmly and assures me that he is counting on my publishing, out of my "wisdom," a comparative lexicon on "mysticités." Then he leads me into his workroom where there are two other persons: a lady music teacher and a literary critic. In one bookcase, volumes on the occult, while in another a skull, a lithograph of the Saint Sulpice type, and a horoscope. The music teacher asks him particulars about a course she intends to offer on "Musical Logic," but she does not know very well what kind of information she needs. Masson-Oursel jots down some observations on a piece of paper, promising to think about them and reply.

Watching him as he listens and takes notes on her questions, I have the impression that I am witnessing in this scene a revelation of his whole life story: an indefatigable, constant curiosity but finding no time to concentrate on the problems that interest him. Multilateral, knowing an enormous number of small and precise things, but really enthused about synthesis. That is why he likes to write very short articles, some just a few pages in length. Probably he doesn't find time, or it seems to him useless, to concentrate, to persevere, to exhaust the problem he is discussing.

11 March

After the cold and snow of 1 March, today, suddenly, spring is in the air. On the way to L'Institut de civilisation indienne I discover this simple thing: you can *recognize* spring anywhere, even here, in the neighborhood of the Sorbonne!

12 March

Today I went to the customs office to get the box of books sent from London—all that remained from the year spent in England. Opening the packages, I recalled the spring and summer of 1940, the afternoons spent at the British Museum, the first air raids. . . . I couldn't do anything all day. I would leaf through a book, then replace it in the box. These books are, for me, *concentrated time, history.* I came on an anthology of detective stories, and I reread a short story by Chesterton. I remembered when and under what circumstances I had first read it: on Cromwell Road, between 2:00 and 4:00 A.M., in August 1940, during an air raid. The anti-aircraft artillery made sleep impossible. I was, if not afraid, at least a little worried—worried that if I were to go to bed for the night, the bombing might start in our sector of the city.

I remember the night of September 9–10 when the blitz began. We took shelter at 10.00 P.M. at Vardala's place. His hotel was multistoried and had a fine shelter. Returning home at 2.00 A.M., we found the museum and several neighboring buildings on fire, while the porter didn't dare look us in the eyes because, as he admitted later, he had suffered a "terrible shock" when incendiary bombs had fallen a few meters from the building.

15 March

Leafing through the books from London. . . . I reread *Cumean Gates* by Jackson Wright, with all the notes I made in it about the labyrinth. I was planning then, in May of 1940, to write a book, *Anthropocosmos;* I had collected a great deal of material, and I believe I understood how the problem had to be put in order to reveal the profound meanings and structural solidarity among all those symbols, rites, and beliefs connected with the labyrinth, the *mandala,* the founding of cities, the orientation of battlements and fortifications, the homologizing of caves with the geography of the underworld, etc.—but I wrote almost nothing.

27 March

I present a paper at L'Institut de civilisation indienne on the vocabulary and techniques of Yoga. Before me are Puech, Jeanmaire, Ph. Stern, M. Leenhardt, Masson-Oursel, and several dozen students and professors, among them Jacques Bacot. I met Bacot in Calcutta in the summer of 1931 at the Library of the Asiatic Society. Van Manen introduced us. He still looks the same. And now, as in 1931, he seems to have descended from another world: *La Vielle France.*

6 April

Yesterday—at the home of Paul Vulliaud, author of the two-volume work *La Kabbale juive,* which had such an importance for me in adolescence. A handsome and haughty old man, at odds with almost everyone.

I found out about Ilarie Voronca's suicide and the crisis that preceded it. He could not escape destiny: for four years he lived in terror of the gas chamber, and now, one year after victory, he commits suicide—by gas!

29 May

I receive the first letter from Al. Rosetti. Very pessimistic as to all that concerns me. In the homeland there is nothing to be done. He doesn't think I could obtain a teaching position. It would be better for me to settle in India, etc.

6 June

This evening, invited to dinner at Louis Renou's, I meet Paul Mus, just back from Indochina (he was still wearing the uniform of a major). He tells me confidentially that the study I published some ten years ago on his extraordinary work, *Barabudur,* helped him very much. At that time the work had not convinced any of the French orientalists; he was depressed over the lack of response to his efforts, and the receipt of the study by a Romanian Indianist had restored his courage (he read the article with the aid of a Romanian-French pocket dictionary he found in a bookstore in Hanoi).

Paul Mus has been at war since 1939. He fought first with a Senegalese regiment in France, then retreated at Dakar, spent two years in India, fought the Japanese in Indochina, was taken prisoner but managed to escape, etc. For seven years he has not opened one scholarly book; he has lived (of course, he didn't use this expression) ''in adventure.'' And thus, as was to be expected, this myopic orientalist eventually surpassed in courage and physical endurance many of his more athletic associates, civilians and soldiers alike.

8 June

Am reading the excerpts from Gide's *Journal* entitled "La Délivrance de Tunis." I wonder to what extent one can keep a journal, properly speaking, in moments of maximum intensity—whether if it is not perhaps more practical to record a few brief notes in a pocket notebook, a few dates, a few key words, a few names. Such a "shorthand" record could be developed later, and it would be more *authentic* than the ennumeration of a great many "concrete details" of a historical situation that is changing so rapidly.

12 June

How curious is the structure of a French university! I attended today the doctoral examination of Jean Filliozat—that young medical doctor who is already a renowned orientalist, familiar with I don't know how many foreign languages including Sanskrit, Tibetan, Tamil, and Kuchean; author of many substantial volumes and essays; secretary of the Asiatic Society; professor for many years at l'Ecole des hautes études. But he did not yet have his doctorate! The chairman of the examining committee, G. Bachelard, expresses surprise that psychoanalysis is absent from Filliozat's dissertation; then the doctoral candidate listens with the patience of an angel to the observations of Jules Bloch, Renou, Masson-Oursel, and E. Benveniste bearing on the more refined philological subtleties. The principal thesis is entitled *La Doctrine classique de la médicine indienne*—yet on the examining committee there is not one historian of medicine!

20 June

Have been laboring for several days to write the study, "Le Problème du chamanisme," promised to Puech for *Revue de l'histoire des religions*. I tell myself that I have no right to keep to myself any longer all I've collected over so many years—almost a thousand pages altogether. Above all, I must present shamanism in the general perspective of the history of religions rather than as an aberrant phenomenon belonging more to psychiatry (for that reason, I shall concentrate on Ohlmarks' book, criticizing its methodological presuppositions).

3 July

The third day of terrific heat, after almost two months of rain. It reminds me of my first summer in Calcutta—but there, on Ripon Street, I had a gigantic fan in the room, and the walls were of stone. I work on the study for *Revue de l'histoire des religions* until 3:00 A.M. Tired, exhausted—and yet it's impossible to fall asleep.

13 July

Today Herescu is black with anger. The news from Romania is grave: seventeen thousand arrested. The wave of terror preceding the elections has begun; H. is afraid deportations will start also.

We walk the streets together for three hours. The rain has chased many people away, but in the Latin Quarter and at the Opera they are still dancing. We stop at several cafés and sit without talking. On the way home, on the bank of the Seine, I gaze for a long time at a pale moon resting wearily on a bank of clouds.

14 July

Gloomy weather; rain almost all day. Only at evening does the sky clear. But it is chilly, and there are rather few people on the street. I watch them dancing. A terrible melancholy . . . which the article on shamanism, grown far too long, does not succeed in exorcising. It's past three in the morning, and still I work—sad, without spirit, without making progress.

17 July

At Montmorency, the guest—along with Cioran and Giza—of the congenial Maxime Némo. Only fourteen kilometers from Paris, only twenty minutes from Gare du Nord, and I feel as though I were at a bathing resort. Those few hours spent at Némo's, the stroll around the little town, the many villas at which we look with admiration and melancholy, the fine, penetrating rain, the sun that appeared toward evening in a sky unbelievably blue after three days of rain—I don't know how to account for the feeling of a "different time" that dominated me all day. When I took the last bus from Gare du Nord to Saint-Germain-des-Prés, I had the impression I was returning to Paris after being away for at least a week.

We saw the famous house of Jean-Jacques Rousseau. It is a ruin, with the roof split open, beams fallen after so much rain, the tapestries torn, and the garden overgrown with nettles and other weeds. From the second-floor window one can see the Eiffel Tower and Sacré Coeur. Visiting the rooms, Cioran and I examine the old magazines. The latest were from 1928–30. We amuse ourselves reading news stories about foreign affairs.

I should like to know more about Jean-Jacques than what I learned the summer of 1922 or 1923 when I read *Emile,* taking copious notes. It was an exceptionally torrid summer. I read in the basement room of our house on strada Melodiei. But even there it became hot, and I was continually cooling my head and chest with water from the bathtub. I worked almost nude. After *Emile* I read the *Confessions* and then began *La Nouvelle Heloise.* I wanted to write several articles—five or six—for *Ziarul științelor populare* which would "exhaust" the subject; then I'd never return to Rousseau, at least not in that periodical. I told myself, probably, that if I had worked so hard and had suffered so much from the terrible, unbelievable heat of that summer vacation time, then at least something *definitive* ought to come of it!

18 July

The young man, O. Vuia, just arrived from Freiburg, gives me a lot of information about Heidegger, who was his professor for six years. It is not true that he had a nervous breakdown; he went to a sanatorium to rest (actually, more for political reasons). He has written an immense book on Nietzsche, and many other things, but he is not publishing anything for the time being for fear of being misunderstood—as he declares he has been misunderstood up until now by Waehlens, Sartre, and all the others.

Since hearing this, I keep asking myself, to what extent does a great philosopher have the right to invoke such a motive; that he won't be understood.

19 July

Religious man tends periodically toward archetypes, toward "pure" states; hence the tendency to return to the first moment, to the repetition of that which was *at the beginning*. So long as the "simplifying," "archetypizing" function of *returns, repetitions,* and *rebeginnings* is not understood, we will not understand how religious experience and the continuity of divine forms are possible—in a word, how it is possible to have *history* and *form* in "religion."

20 July

Since finishing "Le Problème du chamanisme" four days ago, I feel like a schoolboy on vacation. Free, open, at liberty, without a daily schedule. I've been working on that study ever since May. Before that I worked on *Techniques du Yoga* and before *that* on *Prolégomènes*. Thus, only now do I have a feeling of vacation, of freedom, of Paris.

But I must defend myself from the temptation of literature! It would be absurd for me to get involved in writing a novel in Romanian—for readers of "tomorrow."

21 July

He came again this evening—the old adventurer with the beard. When I first met him, I didn't know how much to believe of all he told me: that we are "colleagues," he being an orientalist and professor at the University of Rome; that he has been to Afghanistan and Indochina and took part in the "resistance" in Italy; that Mistral had written about his first volume of poetry, etc. But after an hour I understood—and I felt sorry for him; he is struggling to earn a living for himself and his family—his second wife and several small children are in Italy where he expects to be named to a new academic-diplomatic post. When I asked him whether he knew anything about Papini, he replied in amazement that he had died long ago, that he was a writer of the nineteenth century! And so on and so forth: about Amanulah, about the post he held at Saigon, about the memorial he forwarded to General de Gaulle, about his crossing over into the American lines. . . .

This evening 8:30 came, and still he had not left. We had almost nothing in the house to eat (a few tomatoes, a sardine, two apricots), and after dinner Mihai N. was coming, whom I had not seen in a long while. My poor "colleague" was "hanging around," as they say, for dinner. I had the cruelty to dress, pretending I was going to eat with friends, and leave the apartment with him. We parted, and I returned home stealthily, feeling terribly ashamed of myself. I might have invited him to share my tomatoes, sardine, and apricots, but for some reason his mythomania and his false, strident eloquence were unbearable to me this evening. What drove me out of my mind was *boredom:* I couldn't listen to him any longer; all he was saying was dull, false, uninteresting.

Later, of course, I regretted it.

22 July

Brice Parain tells me that *Techniques du Yoga* will go to to press in October. At that time too I'll receive a sizable advance.

25 July

Walking this evening along the bank of the Seine between Chatelet and the Louvre, I stopped at every ship anchored by the quay, and, seeing a vase of flowers, a pot of beans cooking, and a smokestack smoking sleepily, I was prompted to relive disconnected moments from my adolescence and youth. "Relive" is too weak a word; I deliberately evoked them, I cherished those moments separated in time but linked together by their having the same "subject": river and steamship. I remember a voyage on the Danube between Brăila and Tulcea in 1921 with a few friends, Boy Scouts. As evening fell, I found it pleasant to stare at the yellow waves half-consciously, possessed by a secret joy impossible to confess to the others, because I believed at that time (being under the spell of the first books I had read about Mesopotamia) that I was sailing on the very waters of the Euphrates! . . . Then I passed, almost without a transition, to my first trips on the Ganges, near Calcutta. I saw again, with astonishing clarity—as I have seen it repeatedly since 1932—the bridge over the Hoogly opposite the Calcutta railway station. Then, the cruise on the Rhine in 1937 from Heidelberg to Cologne, the memories of which I tried to "save" by recording on the spot in a pocket notebook all sorts of concrete details as well as everything passing through my mind related to those details.

14 August

Al. Rosetti comes to see me in the course of the afternoon, and we have another long conversation in my room. As always, he is pessimistic; he tells me I must forget I'm Romanian, write only in French, get used to the idea that I'll never return to the homeland, etc. Who'd be interested in Romania, Romanian culture, and Romanian literature?

22 August

The drought in Romania, which I had heard about some time ago but which the papers today describe as an unprecedented catastrophe, upsets and depresses me. Even the Cosmos is our enemy. . . .

23 August

After the assassination of Garcia Lorca, the government of Madrid wanted to execute in reprisal an artist suspected of pro-Franco sentiments. Munoz Seca, an actor and satirist, was chosen—a man who had made fun of everyone including the governmental officials. When they came to arrest him, Munoz Seca exclaimed: "You can take all my goods, and you can take away my freedom, but there's one thing you can never take from me: the terrible fear I've felt ever since you opened that door!"

To my amazement—because I thought I knew "the Spanish soul"— the actor was, nevertheless, shot. Not immediately but six months later.

27 August

I don't believe I'm the only one who can transcend repeated failures and melancholic, hopeless sufferings when, by an effort of

lucidity and willpower, I understand that they represent, in the immediate, concrete sense of the word, a *descensus ad infernum*. Once you
"wake up" *realizing* that you are wandering in an infernal labyrinth,
you feel anew, tenfold, those spiritual powers you considered long since
lost. In that moment, any suffering becomes an "initiatory ordeal."

28 August

Several bad days of extreme fatigue. Insomnia—and in the
morning I am wakened by all sorts of noises coming from this vast,
mysterious building on rue des Saints-Pères in which the apartment—
three-fourths unfurnished—of the proprietor is also located. Someone
is listening to the 8:00 radio newscast, or the concierge comes ringing
at all the doors to deliver the mail, or army trucks stop directly in front
of our windows. Recently the son of the proprietor has come back from
vacation: a young man of twenty-two, bronzed and blythe, who roams
the house in his pajama bottoms, sings, and uses the telephone
constantly. Since he arrived, I haven't felt at home any longer, but rather
as though I were a guest in the house of strangers, and I have the
sensation all the time that I'm disturbing them.

Last night I made an attempt for the first time to sleep with wads of
wax stuffed into my ears. Initially, a bizarre sensation—that I'm cut off
from the world, *alone,* while all around me strange things are
happening. I remove the wax every five minutes: quiet. I put it in again
and I hear improbable noises: a mosquito approaches and buzzes around
me (as I heard on the first nights in Calcutta), a train, groans, fragments
from the second Brandenburg Concerto. But I stubbornly persist—and
at last I succeed in going to sleep with my ears stopped.

31 August

Again that strange dream, of which I can remember nothing
except a crushing sadness, a sadness so totally and transparently
revealed that, in the depths of sleep, my entire being seemed exhausted
with weeping. I know that I found myself in a landscape already
familiar, with many lakes. There, in a series of events I can't recall, *I
repossessed my entire life as a "past" that had become present again.*

Very hard to reproduce here, even approximately, the paradox of that revelation; but I knew that the sadness which overwhelmed me was not connected with any event, with anything localizable in time or space. Rather, it had to do with a plenitude no longer known, with a total recovery of my whole life which I succeeded in having again *all at one time*—although I *knew* that it no longer *is* but that it is my *past*. In that moment I experienced a new dimension of sadness, impossible to bear. Without actually shedding tears, I wept as I have never done in my waking life.

1 September

Emil Cioran doesn't understand my interest in the "objective aspect" of religions. His only interest is in the personal, existential modalities of the various saints, mystics, and bodhisattvas.

An attitude, of course, as modern as can be. Take, for example, the success of Existentialism. But I wonder whether, in this existentialist, "personalistic" obsession, one cannot decipher also something else, namely, the finding in oneself of a dimension lost by modern men—the cosmological. Prior to the Renaissance (and, from then on, exclusively on popular planes) man felt himself integrated into a Cosmos which he assumed and expressed in macanthropic images. All kinds of existential modalities were lived, then, on a cosmic plane. For modern man, such experiences can seem "alien," "objectivized," but for the man of traditional societies there exists a perfect *porosity* between all cosmic planes. The experience of a starry night, for instance, is equivalent to a very intimate, personal experience on the part of a contemporary individual. By projecting himself or homologizing himself with everything, the pre-Renaissance man did not betray himself; he did not "alienate" himself in the Heideggerian *man:* There is nothing "impersonal" (in the sense the term has acquired in Existentialism) in the whole anthropocosmic experience of the man of archaic and traditional societies. The reason I am so eager to decipher symbols and specify the modalities of these societies is because I rediscover in them, diminished and "interiorized," all the nostalgias and enthusiasms I find in modern man.

6 September

. . . The summer has passed without my succeeding in doing any serious work on *Prolégomènes*. It's true the month of August was confiscated by friends, expended in visits and disucssions. But, on the other hand, contemporary history is not designed to stimulate me. War, according to almost unanimous belief, seems inevitable. Time limits are given too: at the latest, 1949 or 1950. . . . Some days I have the feeling I'm wasting my time whenever I work on a book whose appearance isn't imminent. This is the destiny of our generation, immobilized and sterile since 1938. Who in Romania has done anything important or funda-mental since that year?

And yet the imminence of a new conflict ought to stimulate me to finish at least the works begun, because, basically, the duty of any man is to *do* that which he knows he can do *well*.

7 September

I run across a notebook I carried with me in May and June of 1938 in Bucharest. I hadn't looked through it in a long time, and every notation reminds me of certain situations or problems that preoccupied me then. My passion at the beginning of that summer was the reintegration of contraries, a subject I treated in a series of articles in 1938, republished in the little book *Mitul reintegrării* [The Myth of Reintegration] (1942). Other notes were elaborated in 1939. But there are so many more that deserve to be pondered, developed, and reworked in several essays. For instance, there is all that I wrote concerning the concept of physiology propounded by the Romantic medical doctor Göress, who dared to assert: "The object of physiology is to demonstrate the projection of the architecture of the worlds into the organism, and to transport the individual relationships of life into great Cosmic relationships, so that the intuition can grasp here too the most universal relationships of the concrete and thus be able to *read,* brightly and clearly, in those things that are hidden here below in the darkness of terrestrial matter." Or there are these observations relative to Novalis: the regeneration of nature through man; the fecund, mystical meaning of death; the passion for death, which he identifies, quite correctly, with Eros, with the totality of Life. You love the night because you want to free yourself from "individuality." Every reintegration is a "totalization."

8 September

At Dr. Paul Rivet's. Sunday is his day to receive guests. About twenty people, the majority of them South American and Spanish republicans. But I meet not a single ethnologist.

Unforgettable twilight, seen from the window of Rivet's office on the top floor of the Musée de l'homme. "Mira ahora!" shouts old Rivet, and we all hasten to the window, to see the sun emerging from the clouds, still bright enough to set the colors of Paris on fire.

10 September

After browsing through Henry Miller's two *Tropics,* I am not at all convinced of the worth of this writer. The pornography is drowned in a sea of salacious and prententiously nihilistic prose. Basically, Miller thinks he goes to the "ultimate extreme" if he writes and repeats all those words people speak secretly. The despair he pretends to know is merely a seminal exhaustion. I fear he is an unsuccessful writer who has tried to gain fame and success through scandal—and has succeeded.

18 September

At the exposition "Foucauld l'africain" (at les Invalides). A detail I had ignored and which will interest Romanians: Charles de Foucauld belonged to the Plevna (Pleven) officers, class of 1876–78. I admire the meticulousness of his manuscripts. He slept only five hours per night. An admirable landscape by Hoggar; I catch myself dreaming of Berber Africa, the Sahara, and many other such unknown places. Thrilled by the "ruptures of plane" in Foucauld's life: from the undisciplined officer, "full of life," to the austere and chaste researcher; then Trappist monk, then gardener, missionary, and hermit. I understand his craving for solitude. I understand the Trappist experience and even his "adventure," as he called his career as a gardener near the Carmelite hermitage. What I find hardest to understand is his missionary activity. It would be difficult for me to exchange the contemplative life of a Trappist for the tortures required for the converting of a few Tuaregs to the catechism.

20 September

In a speech at Zurich, Churchill calls for the federalization of the European states (only those of western Europe, of course!), and he preaches the reconciliation of France with Germany, whose "spiritual grandeur" he discovers. When we, those few eastern Europeans who can still speak freely, suggested the same thing, we were viewed with suspicion and almost accused of Nazism. . . . But it is nonetheless thrilling to hear Churchill, author of the aerial offensive against the German cities, speaking so touchingly about the "spiritual grandeur" of Germany!

22 September

My enthusiasm for private diaries made me buy a copy of Ramuz's *Journal,* but after turning a few pages I've begun to regret my purchase. Actually, not everyone can keep an interesting and significant journal. The talent of the writer in this case plays almost no role. You either have the "knack" for a private diary or you don't, just as you have it or not for a novella or a fantastic story. For instance, Julien Green is always fascinating, even when recording insignificant details. He is "made" for that sort of writing; you sense his delight as he walks the streets of Paris and sees again certain paintings at the Louvre; you feel his emotion as he recalls happenings from childhood; but above all you discern his need to save concrete time—those irreversible seconds of twilights, of evanescent shadows, laden with revelations. Gide, likewise, fascinates me through all he says about the profession of writing. Even those more vacuous pages from his last journal can be read, although they afford nothing new: so many banal details and mediocre observations seen ennobled by virtue of the simple fact that they were recorded, that they were "written."

25 September

At the Louvre today I content myself with Veronese's *The Descent from the Cross*. Am obsessed for a long time by the yellow clothing of the Lord's Mother. How much wisdom, how much courage the artist shows in this composition: the figures grouped entirely on the left side of the canvas, leaving half the picture almost free, dominated by the sky, as if the artist wished to separate ''Nature'' from ''miracle,'' Cosmos from History.

26 September

Perhaps on account of the sudden outburst of heat like midsummer, I wasn't able to work at all the whole day today. Went to Emil Cioran's. Among other things he told me that he has been tempted more than once to burn his books and manuscripts, in order to commit some *irreparable* act against himself.

. . . It's almost midnight and I can't bear to give up. I feel as though I've robbed myself, letting a whole day pass without writing a line. I've just come home from a neighborhood cinema where I saw a second-rate movie. The windows are open; it's hot, like a summer night. I *must* start writing, in spite of all obstacles and discouragements. . . .

2:00 A.M. Have written three pages. I'm content, because I have ''seen'' the conclusion of the chapter. And it's the first chapter of *Prolégomènes,* the one that has given me the most trouble.

27 September

Hot, and the sky is too clear: a summer day. At the Luxembourg Gardens, I hear the diplomats' automobiles being called over the loudspeaker. I stop a moment to watch the Chinese delegation's car passing. On rue Bonaparte the chestnut trees are already golden-brown, and too many leaves have fallen for me not to sense autumn, however hot it may be outside. In the window of the Picard Bookstore—the same books, faded by the sun. It was on this very bench that I sat talking with Emil Cioran on the first night after my arrival in Paris.

But as I stroll through this neighborhood of St. Sulpice, I cannot control my melancholia and irritation in front of windows displaying religious objects. How much fetishism, how much degeneration into vulgar sentimentalism and infantilism! All those mangers with babies and wise men, Virgins and saints of plaster standing one beside the other like dolls or lead soldiers in a child's play! How can such infantilized religiosity fail to arouse indignation? I say to myself that, in the case of us Eastern Orthodox, our *icons* have protected us from the fetishism of anthropomorphic images. The pseudonaive naturalism of those statues and dolls reminds me of the dubious Vaishnavite devotion, so frequently overflowing with sentimentalism and eroticism, or of the elementary cult of images in Indian villages. But the Indian concept of hierophanies is more profound than that of the decadent Christainity of today. And yet the missionaries say that the Indians are fetish worshippers, while Christianity is . . . etc., etc. The shop windows in the St. Sulpice neighborhood don't even have the excuse that they were composed for poor "pagans" not yet "enlightened" by the Gospel message. . . .

I wrote long ago in *Prolégomènes* several pages about the meaning of icons and "idols." For a "primitive," the image or the idol participates in the sacred; it embodies it. For the devotions of Catholics under obedience to Saint Sulpice, holy images "narrate" the miracle of the Nativity and the mystery of the Holy Passion in a profane way and on a "common" level. They tell all this as a story for children, not even as a *mythology*. Everything is naturalistic and sugarcoated, "spontaneous" and yet artificial (that false "stylizing" of the face of the Holy Virgin, Jesus, etc.), in order to be understood by the children of well-to-do-parents, clean and well mannered.

1 October

A former student of mine from 1936–38, Mihail Şora, reminded me today of the disastrous impression I made on Schileru in 1936 when I went to Brăila to deliver a lecture. Schileru was at that time a lycée pupil. He met me at the station and Mihail Sebastian introduced us. I know that the three of us took the tram and that the boy kept talking to me constantly. He told me, among other things, that in his opinion Aldous Huxley did not write novels but only fictionalized essays, etc. (Sebastian and I amused ourselves later by recalling those "dreadful" things which we ourselves had known in lycée too.) I was in no mood for conversation. Tired from having spent the night on the train, I wanted to be left alone with Sebastian. I had forgotten how I escaped from Schileru. Şora reminded me, because he had it straight from Schileru: while Schileru had all sorts of illusions about his meeting with me and was trying to create a favorable climate, that is, a "spiritual" one, between us—I turned to Sebastian and asked: "Where can you get a good bowl of fish soup here in Brăila?" The poor boy collapsed.

I believe I was wrong to behave like that. But it wasn't my fault if the overly learned adolescent happened to meet me at an "unspiritual" moment!

October

For some time before I fell asleep last night I was tempted again by a play which I "saw" one evening while walking alone on the deserted terraces of the Estoril in December 1944. Sometimes the temptation is so strong that I lie for more than an hour with my eyes open in the darkness, following the characters, listening to them, trying to make out their faces more clearly. If I were to start, I believe I could write it in a few days. But I've promised myself to do nothing else until I've finished the first chapter of *Prolégomènes*.

4 October

An afternoon lost in the hallways of the prefecture, waiting in line for my identity card. I arrived before 2:00, but I succeeded in getting my card only at 5:00—the *last one*. At least fifty people were ahead of me. . . .

I have bought Charles du Bos's *Journal 1921–23*. From the preface I learn that du Bos kept a diary from 1908 to 1921 also but that the manuscripts were illegible, even to himself. For that reason the published text begins with 1921; in that year du Bos started dictating his journal. This explains everything. It is really more of a studio exercise, a pre-essay. Almost always interesting, of course, because he dictated it—but never intimate, allusive, succinct. I have the impression that I'm reading pages from *Approximations*. The first thirty pages are devoted to Amiel. Admirable. For instance, concerning Amiel's style: "Il y a quelques fois jusqu'à l'image tout à fait banale, jusqu'à la chromo-lithografie; il lui a toujours manqué cette épuration de goût par le contact incessant avec les chefs-d'oeuvre de la peinture grâce a laquelle peu à peu de telles images ne se présentent même plus a l'esprit" [It is there sometimes even in the most banal image, even in the chromolithography; he always lacked that refinement of taste that comes through continuous contact with masterpieces of painting—thanks to which, little by little, such images no longer even present themselves to the mind] (p. 14). Also about Amiel: "Le côté *distinction banale*" [the aspect of *banale distinction*] (p. 16); "Son absence de goût est celle-là même de l'adolescence. . . . Son goût unit a la fadeur de l'enfance la sentimentalité de la premiere vieillesse" [His lack of taste is the same as his lack of adolesence. . . . His taste combines the sentimentality of early old age with the tastelessness of childhood] (p. 19).

8 October

For two days it has been clear but cold. Fall came so quickly that it seems natural to be making plans for Christmas.

Admirable observation by Percy Lubbock, which Charles du Bos records in his *Journal:* "Le livre ou l'article que l'on n'est pas en train de faire, que l'on se propose de faire après, est toujours le seul arbe en fleurs de verger de l'esprit" [The book or article which one is not in the process of writing, which one proposes to do later, is always the only tree in bloom in the orchard of the spirit]. I have always been fonder of the book I was planning than the one I was being forced to work on at the time.

9 October

It's getting colder and colder. The wind last night broke the strange web an enormous spider had woven between the top of the lamppost and the board fence of the unfinished building on rue des

Saints-Pères. I would often stop, especially toward evening, to follow the slow, elegant spinning of the spider on that improbable isthmus of thread and dust some two meters above the sidewalk.

At the Louvre for Caravaggio's *Death of the Holy Virgin,* which I had never viewed attentively before. The painting loses much because of its lack of relief in the foreground, especially in the case of the group on the left. The faces are hazy, without "weight." But the Virgin is impressive: a face blighted by suffering, slightly pacified by the touch of death, and that extraordinary falling hand; the sad gold of that divine corpse resting on the folds of the warmest shades of red.

10 October

I must make a great effort to finish the first volume of *Prolégomènes* by 31 December. Then I'll be free and able to return to literary creation. These past years in which I have written so little fiction have diminished and impoverished me. But the fear that any novel or novella I might write would remain in file folders for many years to come paralyzes me. It seems so useless to spend my time on a "work" that no one will ever read. . . .

11 October

I receive from Bucharest *Revista Fundaţiilor Regale* for 1945–47, and I read with greatest excitement the pages from Mihail Sebastian's journal. They are from 1936, when he wrote his first play, *Jocul de-a vacanţa.* A lot of hazy memories, half-forgotten, acquire firmness again: his trips to Breaza, whenever he had a few days free, to work on the play; conversations with Ionel Teodoreanu at Ghilcoş; etc. I can't identify the persons hidden behind the initials. I'll never know the names of the women he loved. Mihai was exceptionally discreet. . . .

How I pitied him for his tremendous efforts, for all the suffering every page cost him! . . . I shall never forgive myself for not going to see him again in August 1942 when I returned to Bucharest for a week. I was ashamed of myself at that time—a cultural attaché in Lisbon—and of the humiliations he had suffered because he had been born and wished to remain Iosif Hechter. Now, in vain, I agonize, too late.

12 October

Last evening I suffered a terrible fit of despondency, provoked probably by reading Sebastian's journal and the notes of Dr. Ulieru, published in *Revista Fundațiilor Regale*. The reading revealed to me all at once my estrangement from my *true* vocation: to be a *Romanian* writer. For several hours I had the feeling that these last six years of living abroad have separated me from the sources of my creativity, have diverted me from the course predestined for me, and that whatever I may do from here on, those six years are irretrievably lost. Moreover, that they have set me on a road from which I cannot return. The terror of the irreversible! For the first time in my life I could *see* and *accept* myself as a failure. . . .

I receive from Ananda Coomaraswamy a letter, the first since 1940. He informs me that he is sending me his books and articles published in the interim and that he is looking forward to meeting with me in the United States during 1947–48. Because, he adds, in December of 1948 he will return permanently to India. That is, he adds, he will leave as soon as he reaches his seventieth birthday. He will give up writing, publishing, and all contact with the world and culture, to enter on the last stage of life which Indian tradition knows, *vanaprasthā:* withdrawal, isolation "in the forest."

13 October

The day before yesterday I had a bad morning. Two detectives came to investigate the case of a Ukrainian man found dead (they didn't tell us where). The only clue: a calling card without any name but with our address: 55 rue des Saints-Pères. They asked the concierge what foreigners were living there permanently, and he sent them to our apartment. When Mme. Chernass, Giza, and I registered surprise, the detectives found this very strange. One of them, smiling meaningly, observed: "I'm not very good at geography, but it's odd: I know that Russia, the Ukraine, and Romania are neighbors!" The landlady, who is Russian, and we Romanians were intimidated. How we dreaded the thought of being hauled in by the police, of making statements, of giving the names of French citizens we know! I imagined the faces of Dumézil, Renou, and the others when they would be called for questioning concerning a Ukrainian corpse with the address of Mircea Eliade! . . .

In confidence, B. S. told Cioran: "The greatest Soviet musician has come to Romania and has played *Carmen*(!) on the violin."

A Soviet journalist, a woman, has established herself in Romania also. B. S. asked her what made her abandon the excellent position she had had in Moscow. "I was fed up with writing the same article for twenty years!" she replied.

The professor of art history at the University of Moscow claims that the last great French painter was Corot.

B. agrees that Marshall Antonescu has become a myth. The stenographic record of the last session of the Tribunal was destroyed, so extraordinary did Antonescu's defense seem to the judges.

15 October

I begin to see the specter of poverty before me. The reserves with which I came to France, accumulated from the sale of my library in Lisbon and from savings made during the winter of 1944–45, are exhausted. If I reduce still further my monthly budget, I'll have enough money to last until spring. After that I shall have to start selling things: a gold bracelet, shoes, clothes, books. But until spring I'm counting on advances from Gallimard and on translations and talks for the B.B.C., work which Cristea spoke to me about. If nothing succeeds, I'll have to give up scientific work and try something else: articles, translations, or even some kind of "job" (I've been told that Ripolin hires intellectuals who are without any "experience").

16 October

I am awakened this morning by the judiciary police who have come for the questioning. I see the form on which our address was written and the word "Ukrainian"; also photographs (the place where the body was found, etc.). Mme. Chernass, Jacques Chernass, Giza, and I are questioned in turn. This examination lasts until 12:00, but the questioning resumes again at 2:30 and continues until 4:30. In the meantime, L. C. rings the bell. Giza tells him "Police!" and he scampers off. The presence of police, interrogations, and searches gives me a feeling of total insecurity.

Afterward, en route to the bookstore Les Belles-Lettres to buy some books for Anton Golopenția, I find myself thinking about my play (*Eurydice?*) with an intensity that almost makes me ill. But suddenly I "see" the plot changing, and in a way that doesn't suit me. In order to be able to wrap it up, I take another walk, and when I return at 7:30 I have the play written in my mind from the first scene to the last. But at home I find Anton, who invites me to dinner and then to the cinema. Otherwise, I'd have begun to write, because I've decided, from this day forward, to work on whatever I'm in the mood for and to stop torturing myself, to stop forcing myself to continue books planned and started long ago which no longer interest me.

17 October

Today, during the inquiry, one of the young detectives discovers my Russian-English dictionary.

"In other words, you know Russian!" he exclaims.

Calmly I show him the other dictionaries—Sanskrit, Greek, German—and explain: "I'm a comparatist."

"Ah, good! In that case . . .

I don't know what he meant by that.

. . . At twelve midnight I began the play. By 1:30 I had written three pages. I stop, dazzled by the discoveries I'm making.

21 October

It is hard to work with two or three visitors coming every day, but I *am* working!

25 October

Bad night. Insomnia until 4:00 A.M. I hear the mouse in the room again. Looking for something to eat, probably. He hunts in all the corners. Exhausted, I stuff some Boulles Quies in my ears and fall asleep. I sleep that way, "sealed up," until 11:00. Then, my first walk in weeks along the Seine. The cold of recent days has suddenly yellowed and thinned the leaves on the plane trees. Almost all the ivy has fallen. I stop before the window of an antiquary shop on rue Bonaparte to look at a Utrillo. But I wonder as I stand there, is this one of the thirty-five hundred authentic canvases by the painter, or does it belong to the *thirty thousand* perfect imitations which have been circulating for several years around the globe, thanks to the diligent labors of an admirer? I like the rejoinder the copier made at his first interrogation: "I prefer copying 'classics' rather than painting mediocre things in keeping with my vision and potential."

26 October

Rainy, sad, dark. After lunch I go to the Société Asiatique to return some borrowed books, and I return with others. Browsing through them at home, I inoculate my soul with the poisonous passion for erudition. Then Herescu comes, and we talk until 5:00. Half an hour later, I turn on the lamp and begin to transcribe act 1. I'm not in the mood for it, but I know that if I break off the writing for a day or two, my poor play risks having to wait several years to be finished. This is the explanation for the many, many things begun—from Indistics, history of religions, and folklore to philosophy, novels, and plays—which lie abandoned in my files. Once I caught myself saying, actually, what a good thing it would be if a fire. . . .

28 October

Yesterday and today I did no work at all. Too many visitors, too many business matters—and my interest in the play has dwindled almost to the zero point. I propose to lay it aside for a few days and then reread all I've written.

I saw Alphonse Dupront, formerly the director of l'Institut français in Bucharest. Very kindly he volunteers to "testify" for me at the Sorbonne, to put a stop to the cabal of Stoilov and his colleagues. He speaks of the work which has engrossed him for several years: the restoration of Western man. He and his associates have organized teams, gone on "retreats," and are planning to make personal contact with all the "elites" of France. It is interesting that the techniques for "self-recovery" which they apply resemble Indian methods. He himself remarked, concerning his own body, that the Westerner must *be incarnated,* must truly *occupy* his physical body, must be incorporated within himself. (I told him that this is the first exercise required in Yoga practice.)

He told me about his illness, especially about the lack of sensation in his legs. He does not feel his feet, calves, or knees, and when he walks he has the strange sensation that he is floating. I remind him in passing (because these things cannot be expressed in words anyway) about Indian exercises for "making sensible" and "occupying" certain "opaque" epidermal regions (soles of the feet, heels, etc.). He agrees that the Orient can teach us this essential thing: the conquest of our own body—but he asks Orientals not to talk philosophy with him, because "we don't have the same theoretical vocabulary."

30 October

I haven't written anything today, but in the rare hours of peace and quiet (when I had no visitors) I thought about *Aventura spirituală* (which probably will be the title of the play). I ask myself why I should not have the courage to combine comedy and fantasy here too, in drama, as I've done in certain novellas and novels.

31 October

Bostanian told me when he came to see me that once, in Spain, he had to hide, by himself, a chest containing four hundred kilos of gold. He took it by car to a country villa which he had rented some time previously. In the middle of the night he dug a hole and dragged the chest to it on wooden runners, while trembling for fear that some neighbor might be watching him. Then, lifting it with a lever, he let it slide into the hole and buried it.

I had the impression I was listening to the improbable confession of an assassin.

* * *

This afternoon I resumed work on the play at act 2, and by 1:00 tonight I have written twelve pages. It will take just one more page to finish the act, but I'm stopping for fear of disturbing its beauty.

1 November

I explained to a young Romanian born and reared in a small provincial city what the Criterion group meant in Bucharest during the years 1933–37, and to what extent the popularity enjoyed then by those young writers and philosophers can be compared with the Existentialist vogue in Paris today. Like J.-P. Sartre, Camus, and Simone de Beauvoir, the members of Criterion expressed themselves on multiple planes: public lectures, articles in weekly reviews and newspapers with large circulations, novels, philosophy, literary and dramatic criticism, and aesthetics. Criterion signified the passing over into culture of the "university moment," the descent of the intellectual into the arena, his direct contact with the public, with the youth in particular—exactly what the Parisian Existentialists have attempted and have succeeded in doing. Sartre has a "philosophical system" which he imposes; we did not have one, but the majority of Criterionists were "existentialists" of sorts without knowing it. What interested them above all was "authenticity," direct experience, the autobiographically "concrete": hence their passion for private diaries, "confessions," and "documents." If Criterion had had an instrument of expression other than the Romanian language, it would have been considered the most interesting precursor of the French Existentialism of today.

3 November

I could not begin writing until 10:00 tonight. This afternoon I transcribed act 2. Am working now on Act 3, which seems to me the most difficult one.

6 November

I worked last night until 5:00 A.M. in order to transcribe act 4. And yet I can't believe that the play is finished!

7 November

Anticlimax. Melancholy, fatigue, detachment—from the play, from literature, from life. I had planned to reread the entire play and to write here, in this notebook, my final interpretation—the only one that seems valid to me. But I'm unable to do anything—even be amused. I went to a neighborhood cinema, but I kept yawning the whole time.

10 November

This evening I reread the play. Dissatisfied with act 1, content with the acts 2 and 3, enthusiastic about act 4.

12 November

Am working at simplifying act 1. I believe I've learned one thing: that a good text has to be written three times (to be elaborated later). It's no use trying to deceive myself. I must devote at least five to six weeks to a play. But since I'll never have that much time to myself again, all at once, I must give up the whole idea. . . .

13 November

Vuia tells me today that Heidegger, when he was expecting to be radically purged as a "Hitlerite," pointed to a stack of manuscripts and said: "If the Germans bring me such an insult, I'll burn all my unpublished works" (which are, they say, the most interesting ones).

14 November

An orgy of reading relative to the *Prolégomènes,* lasting until 2:00 A.M.

15 November

Today I receive my first money earned as author's royalties in France: four thousand francs, from Gallimard, representing the first monthly payment on the book *Techniques du Yoga.*

25 November

Yvonne Wright takes me today to the home of Robert Desoille, the inventor of psychosynthesis. I knew nothing about him except for the chapter Bachelard devoted to him in *L'Air et les songes* and except for the first thirty pages of his own book, *Le Rêve éveillé,* which I bought only this morning. Desoille interests me because he used the technique of dreams of ascension, utilizing the symbolism of flight, climbing, etc.—that is, precisely the symbols, myths, and rituals which I myself discussed in "Le Problème du chamanisme." Thus, he has cured neuroses and other kinds of mental illness by using (without knowing it) elements of shamanistic rituals and symbols of ascension (which, as I have shown in my study, are something entirely different from "primitive" magical practices). I wanted to learn more about the method he employed. Unfortunately, Desoille lost his wife a year ago, and since then he hasn't been the same. According to Mme. Wright, his wife sustained him, gave him courage, assisted him in all his experiments. Now, left alone, Desoille finds support only in Communism. He preaches Marxism like a Saint Francis. He believes the Russian Revolution will free humanity from evil, sin, and ignorance. Just now he is writing a book: *Le Rêve éveillé et le marxisme.* We talk for some time about yoga, occultism, and psychoanalysis. However, I leave disappointed. He is a very good man, with great sensitivity, who is trying to save himself by inventing an "external mysticism."

6 December

This evening at the concert of old music, "Ars rediviva." The unpublished Concerto in C Flat Major by J. M. Leclair fascinates me, as did also his concerto for violins and orchestra I heard last year. I'm becoming increasingly captivated by this French composer of whom I had been completely ignorant. The Bach cantata, "Blieb bei uns," seemed to address me and at the same time to *express* me—the person I am today. I find these concerts organized by Claude Crussard to be like participating again in a spiritual exercise abandoned long ago. "Largo," from the Concerto in G Major by G. P. Telemann, unpublished and performed here for the first time, confirmed for me all that I have learned this year relative to the process of reintegration (about which I shall have to write someday . . .).

7 December

Last night's dream: a moonlit night in a meadow, with many children of about six or seven years of age around me. We are all looking at the moon. Suddenly a cluster of stars of a strange, incomparable beauty begins to fall. The stars come closer and closer; we are afraid they will crush us. Then we see they are falling all around us, like golden apples. But they are smaller and hot. We begin to eat them, but I, holding one that is still burning in my hand, start to run, crying: "Quickly, everyone, take advantage of your opportunity! These are falling stars; they bring us good luck!"

14 December

A few days ago I ran into Theodore Besterman, the director of the Library and Bibliography Division of UNESCO. A long talk about what each of us has been doing for the past six years (the last time I had seen him was in December 1940 at Oxford). Today, after having lunch together, we toured the bookstores and antiquary shops, seeking any book "by or about Voltaire." We were looking especially for the bibliography of his works compiled by Bengesco, which Besterman much admires and of which I once had one volume in Bucharest. (It was purchased in 1922 when I was in the fourth class of lycée. I was reading sixteen to eighteen hours a day and considered myself a Voltairean because I was an "encyclopedist" and had a mania for writing. I admired Voltaire's enormous literary talent, his multilateral genius, and his fantastic bibliography.) Laden with packages, we arrived at the bookstore-café l'Arc-en-Ciel and rested there a half hour, making plans over cups of coffee. I told Besterman frankly that it would be absurd for him to undertake to translate the whole corpus of Voltaire's works but that it would be better to confine himself to his masterpieces. Furthermore, he ought to start to work immediately lest this gigantic plan too should fail (as had other projects of his: for instance, the book about America in four volumes, the monograph on reincarnation, etc.)

15 December

There has come to my attention a *Combat* article about the journals of Gide, Julien Green, and Charles du Bos. The author is surprised that, after taking such pains to observe and analyze himself, the writer of a journal does not reveal himself any more effectively there than in any other book he writes, that at any rate he does not "know himself" and does not confess everything, as we might expect him to do in a confession. Hence, for gaining knowledge of a writer, his journal is less true than his memoirs or a frank autobiography written in the twilight of life.

But I wonder whether that is the purpose of a journal: to know myself better and to reveal myself more boldly to the eventual reader. In lycée I too, like all adolescents, was obsessed with "knowing myself" through a long self-analysis of the genre Amiel. But later, when I reacquired a taste for the journal, something entirely different interested me: to record, in the first place for my own curiosity *later* and for purposes of subsequent verification, a series of details and impressions concerning my life and experiences of those days. Almost never have I felt a need to "confess" myself wholly on a journal page. Besides, I believe a truly frank self-portrait, candid down to the smallest detail, would not be significant unless integrated within an exemplary confession with a certain moral or prophetic import. It seems to me that a journal is better realized (as a literary genre) and more instructive (on an ethical, philosophical, historical plane) if the author records, in the flux of the hours, certain images, situations, and thoughts—if, as I have written on another occasion, he saves, by "freezing" them, fragments of *concrete time*.

17 December

This evening, as I am entering the Café de Flore to buy some cigarettes, I meet Lavastine with a half-drunken companion who introduced himself as the "abbé défroqué surréaliste." He was the first surrealist priest; he walked the streets sometimes in a cassock, sometimes in a robe. I listened to him for a quarter of an hour, trying to follow his train of thought. He spoke first about his journey to India and Tibet (where he discovered Buddhist monks who were in correspondence with Benedictines in Europe), then about Leclerc's division in which he fought. He said something also about an inheritance of fifteen million francs, but I understood later that it was not he who had received this, but a friend. The latter, not knowing what to do with the money, decided to publish a literary review.

As we were about to part, Lavastine recalled 23 August 1944, when, in a room with Brasillach, Rebatet, and other collaborationists, all very grave, the former abbot began to shout: "Why are you all sitting here, looking gloomy? Take arms and follow me! We'll stop Leclerc's men from entering Paris!" The majority of those to whom these words were spoken were executed or are now in prison. The surrealist abbot, however, claims that he was decorated by Leclerc, "who is a true Christian."

20 December

For many years, as Christmas approaches, I have found it pleasant to read again about the legends, rituals, and customs of the Twelve Days (between Christmas and Epiphany): about the carnival-type ceremonies, the animal masks, legends of headless horses that appear on New Year's Eve, etc. Such myths and ritual scenarios are found not only in Indo-European societies but also in Japan, China, among the Ainu, and in other places. Everywhere, the twelve days that precede the New Year constitute a decisive moment in the life of the community; at that time the souls of the dead visit the living, the initiation of adolescents takes place, etc. All this was known long ago. But why does the return of the dead occur *only,* and *everywhere,* on the eve of the New Year? Because New Year's represents not only the critical moment of the year (the "chaos" that sets in immediately after the conclusion of a temporal cycle) but also a cosmogonic moment. New Year's *repeats* the Creation; with each new year, the world begins again, is reborn—more precisely, is *made anew.* (Take, for instance, the ceremonial recitation, in Mesopotamia, of the Poem of Creation, as well as the ritual reenactment, in Egypt and so many other places, of the

conflict that preceded and established Creation—a scenario that survives in the popular beliefs and customs of southeastern Europe.) In the
interval between the year which is ending (i.e., the Old World which is
disappearing) and the new year (i.e., the Cosmos on the way to being
recreated), the souls of the dead approach the living, because they hope
for a *repetition* (at least an ephemeral one) of existence (they appear
"incarnated" in masks and animals) or because they hope, implicitly, for
an *abolition* of Time, hence for a transcending of their proper condition
as shades. I shall develop all these things in the little book I've been
working on for several weeks, *Archétypes et répétition* (in Romanian I
called it at first *Cosmos și istorie*).

26 December

Last night I met Harold King. Very pessimistic. We will live for
thirty years, perhaps, under the dictatorship of the proletariat, and then
will come the war that will bring the end of our continent. He said to
me: "And all this because of you—you scholars! Because you've put
science into the hands of everyone!"

Well, well, well!*

27 December

Georges Dumézil, who has been kind enough to read and correct
the French translation of *Prolegomene,* expresses to me his enthusiasm
for this book. He predicts that I will be "imitated, plagiarized, and
cribbed." Meanwhile, I still have three chapters left to write. And then
there's the problem of the publisher. Gallimard has asked for it, but I
hesitate. I've been told that they have tons of manuscripts waiting to be
published.

7 January, 1947

At Besterman's, and then to dinner with Mr. and Mrs. Roberts
also, at a restaurant in Montparnasse. Besterman told me the story of
this man Roberts: by age fifty he had written some sixty volumes—of

*English in the original—TRANS.

all sorts and in all fields. He started out with a journey to India at eighteen in search of "the truth"—only half of which Madame Blavatsky's books had revealed to him. His career as a writer he concluded with detective novels, and his career as a saint with cynicism, drunkenness, and facile nihilistic philosophy. Between these two poles he found time to travel in Russia, and he enjoyed being able to discover and photograph Madame Blavatsky's marriage certificate and the birth certificate of her son—thus putting a finish to the legend of the Inspired Virgin. (He wrote a biography of Madame Blavatsky too, of course.)

After dinner Roberts wanted at all costs to convince me that Paris is a dead city, that it is no use protesting the closing of the cafés at midnight—because long before midnight the places are empty anyway. And so we went to the Flore, the Deux-Magots (which he found dull), and then, with his wife still accompanying us (we had taken Besterman home), to the Dupont. We found there, indeed, enough gloom to bring on a neurosis, and it was not yet midnight. "Where are your students who can't continue their discussions of Hegel because the manager throws them out at midnight?"

Indeed, where are they? Only a few tables occupied by palid, unshaven youths, and no impassioned discussions to animate them.

10 January

I shall be moving 1 February, probably into a hotel. My books I plan to store in boxes at a furniture warehouse. When I informed Dumézil of my decision, he exclaimed: "How healthy you are!"

25 January

Guy Bernard spoke this evening at l'Arc-en-Ciel about Egyptian cosmogonic texts, on which he recently passed his doctoral thesis. Taking part in the discussion also was Marcel Griaule, just back from Africa. I was glad to be able to hear him (his book about African masks clarified many obscure things for me). We continued our discussion afterward, *en petit comité,* in Lavastine's library (until 1:30 A.M.). Griaule tells us that he spent I don't know how many years in Africa, having made some fifteen expeditions there in all. He was almost sure he had "understood" the religious and social system of the Dogon and the Bambara. The last time, only six months before he was to leave Africa, he met an old man—who eventually talked to him for a total of one hundred fifty hours, with very brief periods of rest. "And after the fifteenth hour, my whole system collapsed. All I had read and written up to that time began to be shaken. I don't know what to believe; I have the impression now that we are at the turning point in African studies. Those unfortunate Negroes have revealed to me the meaning of the Platonic Logos! Their symbolism is so tremendous and so coherent! Only the study of such an archaic tradition in its living state can help us to understand other, dead religions."

I never imagined I'd find so soon a verification—and from the most illustrious French Africanist—of my whole "theory" about primitive symbolism.

26 January

An almost violent attack of insanity on the part of our unfortunate proprietor obliges us to move tomorrow or the day after, not on 31 January. Forbidden the use of the kitchen, we eat no lunch. We start packing our things. I fill two large trunks with books and pack fifteen more boxes. We work like this, on our knees, till midnight.

28 January

I moved this morning to Hôtel de Suède, 31 rue Vaneau. I have a very spacious room (no. 17). We spent yesterday and the day before cold, terrorized, drinking only tea (because we didn't have access to the kitchen), packing boxes. Finally, this morning we escaped! Giza found a little room at Hôtel de Étrangers, on rue de Beaune. We eat lunch at the Restaurant Pascal, opposite the Senate. This evening we drink tea.

Next door to me, a young family in a mood for talking. Impossible to sleep. I select from the pile of books a volume of Unamuno's *Ensayos*. I reread "Lectura y interpretatión del Quijote," the article which provoked such an uproar when it appeared in *La España modern* in 1905. Unamuno's tirade against Cervantes is fully justified. If he hadn't discovered Don Quixote, Cervantes would have been a fifth-rate writer. Unamuno rightly remarks that *Don Quixote* is the only masterpiece which does not lose—but on the contrary gains—by being translated, since in this way the artificiality and precocity of the style is attenuated. One sees clearly that Cervantes has not understood the hero with regard to all that is grand and exceptional about him. Sometimes the author rushes to express his attitude toward the character—and this attitude is always that of the man on the street, of "common sense." Thus, for example, Unamuno refers to the episode of the discourse on the Age of Gold, the speech the knight delivers to the goatherds, concerning which Cervantes expresses his own opinion, that Quixote is an "inútil razonamiento" [useless rationalist]. But, remarks Unamuno, the goatherds listened to him "embobados y suspensos" [fascinated and astonished], and they repaid Don Quixote with pastoral songs. Therefore *they* understood him, and they liked all they learned about the Golden Age.

31 Janaury

I've continued tonight reading Unamuno's *Ensayos.* "Sobra la erudición y la critica" is a courageous, lucid essay of amazing "timeliness." This evening I reread several articles from *Contra esto y aquello.* Siding with Flaubert against human stupidity, Unamuno writes: "The most modern vulgarity, fashionable vulgarity, vexes me even more than the old, traditional kind. The commonplace of this morning is more irritating than the one of yesterday, because it gives the appearance of novelty and originality. For that reason, anarchistic stupidity infuriates me more than Catholic stupidity" (*Ensayso* 2, p. 974). Excellent!

1 February

At l'Orangerie to see the Vincent van Gogh exposition. Sensational! I knew just the two paintings of his in the Louvre; the rest only in reproductions. For the first time I can *walk* for several hours among nothing but van Goghs. My preferences direct me to the canvases from Arles, in particular the street with the café where the painter lived, and to the orchards. Evident is the influence of Gauguin—but also how much resistance to him! It would be interesting to trace this capacity, peculiar to geniuses, of accepting an influence, of assimilating a technique or an exterior inclination, and yet, even in an "influenced" work, of resisting and reacting against those influences.

3 February

In a plane crash near Cintra, Claude Crussard and eight other musicians of "Ars rediviva" have lost their lives. Seldom has an accident impressed me as has this one. Paris, for me, is left bereft of its most important musical association.

5 February

Yesterday we scarcely saw the daylight at all. When I awoke, the sky was yellow and dark, as the Bengal sky can be on the eve of the monsoon. I could see to work only by the light of the lamp. (Dumézil gave his lecture under artifical lights also, between 10:00 and 12:00.) On the street, people's faces were sallow, sometimes violet. On the way to the Sorbonne where I went to hear Dumézil, I felt that an apocalyptic catastrophe might happen at any moment. The air had become a kratophany.

6 February

I see Al. Rosetti, who arrived on the same official train as did the commission which has come to sign the peace treaty. He is here to deliver three lectures at le Collège de France. All that he tells me about the situation in Romania alarms me. If a representative of the government admits people are dying of hunger, what must it really be like there?!

8 February

This evening at l'Arc-en-Ciel, a lecture by Marcel Griaule about African symbolism. Amazed and almost exhausted by the overwhelming richness of that symbolism, I can stand it for no longer than an hour. I ask myself on the way home, how is it possible for the same people who "see" everywhere the arithmetical symbolism of the Gemini, $4 + 3 + 1$, $7 + 1$, etc., who homologize even the smallest everyday gestures to the Zodiac, to the symbolism of weaving, of metallurgy, and of smelting—how can they fall asleep when asked to count to five? . . . Simply because *counting* doesn't interest them. Very likely a European intellectual would begin to yawn after ten or fifteen minutes if he were forced to puruse the implications of the group 4 + 3 + 1, the basis of the whole mathematical symbolism of the Dogon and Bambara peoples.

9 February

I take advantage of an unexpected and extraordinary, spring-like morning today to revisit the van Gogh exhibition. I identify the canvases painted under the influence of Gauguin. And it seems to me that I can *sense* van Gogh's mannerism in his last stage. Nevertheless, he is a no less admirable painter; he is not afraid of creating almost exaggerated perspectives having a dizzying third dimension, rather than a somewhat artificial space of two dimensions which one has to accept as a creation of his own retinas.

This evening we see O'Neill's *Electra,* with Margaret Jamois and Valentine Tessier. It is abridged and lasts only three hours, but it is so skillfully abridged and so well played that it captivates me, although I had the complete text rather fresh in my mind. What surprises me is the audience—only half-hearted. Tickets were available at the box office as late as thirty minutes before the performance, while at plays on the boulevard you have to buy them several days in advance. And the applause at Le Secret. . . . Giza tells me that when *Electra* played at Bucharest with an almost complete text, people formed lines two hundred meters long, beginning at 8:00 A.M. Moreover, the Russian army was at Iaşi, and several other O'Neill plays were being performed in Bucharest at the same time. Was it only snobbishness? Or is the Romanian public really qualitatively superior and more receptive to masterpieces than is the Parisian public?

14 February

After learning my address from the legation, a young man named Marin comes to see me today. He is an employee at the Ministry of Public Works. No overcoat, with only a beret on his head, he entered the room rather boldly. He had a reason! For four years he has been searching through all the new and used bookshops in Paris and the provinces for a copy of my *Yoga*. In 1944 he saw it advertised in a catalog from a used-book store in Lyon. He took the train and went to buy the book. It had been sold. Finally, a year ago, he made up his mind to transcribe it, page by page, from the copy in the library of the Musée Guimet. But being only a clerk, he had no free time except Saturday afternoons, and he managed to copy only about a hundred fifty pages (notes and all). I assured him that soon a new book of mine would be published by Gallimard and that in a year or two a revised and augmented edition of my old *Yoga* would appear. He was so delighted that he begged me to have an apéritif with him at the corner bistro.

16 February

A wonderful letter from Dinu Noica which purifies, uplifts, and enriches me. "It is our great privilege, we who are without a position, without status on the social plane, to be able to say: my life beings tomorrow."

20 February

From B. C. I receive 30,000 francs, borrowed on long term. The money came just in time. My reserves were exhausted. For three weeks we've been eating lunch in sordid restaurants at less than a hundred francs each, and evenings drinking tea. When someone offers me an American cigarette, I have trouble holding back an infantile squeal of delight.

27 February

G. Dumézil tells me that "Le Problème du chamanisme" is a milestone in the history of religions, and he is glad that he has an article in the same issue of *Revue de l'histoire des religions*. Listening to him, I blush, but I believe there is some truth in what he says; with all its imperfections, my study has the merit of presenting for the first time the phenomenon of shamanism in the only perspective in which it becomes intelligible, that of the history of religions.

1 March

I am awakened by a bright, glaring light. Never have I seen the sun from my window on rue Vaneau so fiery and brilliant. I open the window and let in an icy breath of winter. Why do I feel, nevertheless, so confident, so content? Maybe it's because I worked until quite late last night on chapter 2 of *Archétypes et répétition* and I foresee the ending.

Pawels writes me that "Secretul Doctorului Honigberger" fascinated him and that he believes it "capable of attracting a wide public; but in a good way, because you offer less for amusement than for meditation." But the French translation by J.C. seems to him "very unworthy of what one divines of the original text, and it loosens up the work too much. The style ought to be as elegant and compact as that of Mérimée." Moreover, he doesn't understand the ending very well. . . .

5 March

Joachim Wach, currently professor at the University of Chicago, writes to invite me to conduct a course or a series of lectures for the department of history of religions at his school. If only I could obtain a visa . . . !

11 March

I meet Puech, who congratulates me for "the courage to pose a problem" (he means "Le Problème du chamanisme").

18 March

I read Maurice Nadeau's book, *Histoire du surréalisme*. Amazed by how many problems from the history of religions and oriental studies with which I have wrestled for so many years I find here again (from another perspective, of course) in the writings, concepts, and nostalgias of André Breton. In *Les Vases communicants* he proclaims that the poet knows how "méler l'action au rêve . . . , confondre l'interne et l'externe . . . , retenir l'éternité dans l'instant . . . , fondre le général dans le particulier" [to mingle action with dream . . . , to intermingle the internal and the external . . . , to retain eternity in the instant . . . , to dissolve the general in the particular]. This is precisely what the yogins, tantrics, and many other Eastern "mystics" propose to do (cf. *Techniques du Yoga*). The rediscovery of the everyday miracle (an obsession of Breton) is an attitude familiar to "primitive" religious societies. The surrealists see in their movement not a new literary school but a means of gaining knowledge about "unexplored continents" (the dream, the subconscious); such an ambition can be well understood only by someone who knows oriental techniques of meditation (because what have they pursued but the exploration, domination, and "transmutation" of the dynamisms of the subconscious?). In a manifesto, Breton even speaks about the possibility of fusing "deux états qui ne sont contradictoires qu'en apparence, atteindre la realité absolue, la surréalité" [two states which are contradictory only in appearance, attaining absolute reality, surreality]. I don't know another Western text (recent) that expresses more truly the ancient nostalgia of the Indian spirit, which the yogic and tantric techniques strive to achieve. The obsession for the "total liberation of the spirit" likewise is a characteristic belonging to the whole Indian culture.

5 April

At Musée Cernuschi to see the Ajanta frescoes, marvelously copied by a young Persian painter. The sensuality of those fabulous images, the unexpected importance of the feminine element! How could the Buddhist monk "liberate" himself from the temptations of the flesh while surrounded by all those superb, nude bodies, triumphant in their plenitude? Only in a Tantric version of Buddhism could such a eulogy to woman and sensuality have a place. Someday it will be understood what an important role Tantrism has had, because, among other things, it revealed and imposed on the Indian consciousness the worth of "form" and "volume" (the triumph of the most languorous anthropomorphism over the original aniconism).

10 April

I discover in *Sein und Zeit* several pages about "repetition" which confirm the reflections I made concerning the ontology and anthropology of archaic peoples. An old ambition of mine: to write someday a metaphysics and an ethics using *exclusively* documents from "primitive" and oriental civilizations.

2 May

Virgil Ierunca, recently arrived from Romania, tells me that in our homeland Existentialism is the only political diversion possible, the only anticommunistic resistance tolerated at all. This accounts for its huge success, especially among the youth; this explains also the attacks on the part of the governmental intellectuals (I have no other name for them, because they aren't Marxists or Communists but simply opportunists). Mihail Ralea, in two lectures at the Foundation, attacked the "jabbering" of Kierkegaard and the "Romanian Existentialists," Nae Ionescu, Mircea Eliade, and Emil Cioran.

9 May

I borrow five hundred francs from Emil. If bad luck wouldn't follow me so persistently, and if I didn't have to ask myself every Monday how I'm going to pay my hotel bill at the end of the week, I might be able to finish *Archétypes et répétition.*

12 May

I take the silverware to the pawn shop. With a great effort, I finish chapter 3 of *Archétypes et répétition.* I must resist the temptation to turn this essay into a monograph. Its purpose is to raise problems, not solve them.

13 May

Today Julian loans me fifteen hundred francs; I can pay a week's rent and have enough left for a meal.

* * *

As I progress in my reading of Hegel's *Lectures on the Philosophy of History,* I find "inaccuracies" and misconceptions at every step, but how admirable is this effort to encompass everything, to take everything into account and valorize all things! From time to time Hegel commits errors, whether because the science of his day misled him (for instance, in the case of China and India), or whether he *wanted* or *had* to err in order to be able to integrate (by force!) all those materials he had into his system. But what does that matter? Reading Hegel, not only are you invited to see a meaning in universal history, but above all you see that it is possible to speak of a universal history which is not just a juxtaposition of isolated chapters. How depressing is our excessively fractured and fragmented vision of history! We know, of course, much more than Hegel knew (or wished to know), but who *integrates* this infinite body of knowledge, who realizes *in his own consciousness* that a universal history exists? I oppose with all my strength Hegel's "historic" vision (and in *Archétypes et répétition* I show why), but that doesn't stop me from admiring his oeuvre.

8 June

Under this rain which wakes me in the morning, darkens my day, and ennervates me until well past midnight, stopping only long enough to allow me a glimpse of an autumnal sky—my whole being is somnolent. But is this the fault only of the sudden transition from scorching heat to rain? Or am I so made that a long run of days on which I can work almost constantly for fifteen to sixteen hours with no sense of fatigue is inevitably followed by vegetative days, days in which the most ordinary pages seem hard to write? For many years I've told myself that when I resolve the "mystery" of this alternation, I'll succeed in organizing my production.

13 June

I finish the chapter on the sun and solar religion for *Prolégomènes*. I want to start another chapter (on sacred space), but I *must* at all costs conclude *Archétypes et répétition* by writing that short, final chapter which I keep postponing. (I have, in addition, two articles to write).

21 June

Several days ago doamna N. Cranfil read me an excerpt from a letter she had received from the homeland. In a village by the Danube a peasant woman confessed, in great secrecy, to the one who wrote the letter: "We women have agreed to stop inducing abortions from now on . . . because our race is perishing."

The decision was made at a time when the children of the village were feeding on the flowers of the acacia trees.

23 June

Puech tells me that my request for a grant, sent to the bursar's office at le Centre de la recherche scientifiques, has not come to his hand and that he doesn't know to what section it was assigned but that he will speak to G. Le Bras. Moreover, he has been thinking for some time of arranging something for me, a visiting lecturer's position at l'Ecole des hautes études. "I don't understand why we don't know how to take advantage of our great good fortune in having a man like you in Paris! I have the impression that politics will end up making complete imbeciles of us!" etc., etc.

29 June

I finished last night the study on Dumézil's work, and this evening, by working steadily, I finished transcribing it. Twenty-four pages. And, as usual, I didn't begin writing good French until I was almost done.

30 June

The day before yesterday, in the evening, there was a big storm. As I was going to close a window which opens on the stairs and was threatening to break, one of my neighbors, a very distinguished elderly lady who was once a friend of Maurice Barrès and who has the "cult of the French language," opens her door and calls me to see from her window how the huge trees in the park next to the building were breaking. It was, indeed, a beautiful sight. "Je vis avec cet arbre!" the old lady exclaimed in ecstacy. "Et puis, moi, j'adore la tempête!"

1 July

I reread canto 4 of the *Iliad*. The scene of the duel between Paris and Menelaus is inimitably comic and charming at the same time. Then, having been transported miraculously by Aphrodite into Helen's bedroom, Paris confesses that he has never desired her more than *now*, not even when he possessed her for the first time, after having kidnapped her, on the island of Cranae. Is it only because Aphrodite had inflamed him? Or is it because he had been so close to death and had been afraid—and that the imminence of death had exacerbated all his erotic powers?

7 July

A few days ago I began a new study for *Revue d'histoire des religions:* "Le 'Dieu lieur' et le symbolisme des noeuds." In a way, it is a pretext to illustrate, on the basis of some specific and rather well-known documents, my hermeneutical method.

10 July

At a private meeting at l'Arc-en-Ciel, arranged by Lavastine for the purpose of discussing the lecture schedule for fall, a curious fellow spoke up. Dressed in a shirt that was almost red, seeming younger than his gray moustache indicated him to be, he confessed that for the past ten years he had not read a newspaper or listened to the radio, had neither bought nor read any book (he contented himself with the ten volumes he had chosen in his youth), had not voted and had paid no taxes, had not attended one play or made any visits. Why had he come to l'Arc-en-Ciel? To see whether it has to do with a "true initiation." He stopped going to Notre Dame when he saw the tricolor banner fluttering over the cathedral. "Because this is the flag of a party, not of France!" (For certain, the man is a monarchist.)

At Lavastine's last lecture, I met a doctor who for thirty years had been studying the problem of circumcision. He had reached the sensational conclusion that a "Semitic race" does not exist. "Semites" are created by circumcision—as are also certain Negroes and certain Austroasiatics who, he claims, are of a "Semitic type" and character. All this seemed to me at the time—and still does—fantastic. Today the doctor expounds for a quarter of an hour on the origin of the Mongol race: having poisoned themselves with an excess of ptomaine as a result of their preference for spoiled food, the Chinese *show death* (their skeleton-like heads) by the very form of their faces. The Mongol type is the *cranium made transparent,* the anticipation of a postmortem "situation."

I don't know whether or not there is any truth in such a hypothesis, but how "poetic" it is! To betray your "familiarity with death" through skull-like cheek bones and yellow skin, a condition at which you have arrived not through a spiritual disaster but through a toxicity produced by eating carrion!

13 July

I remember that a year ago at this time I was struggling to finish "Le Problème du chamanisme." I am doing exactly the same thing a year later—trying to complete, today or tomorrow, "Le 'Dieu lieur' et le symbolisme des noeuds." If I hadn't insisted on writing it now, before Puech goes on vacation, how gladly would I have abandoned myself to literature! But, for the time being, literature is forbidden me. I have still to write: the final chapter for *Archétypes et répétition,* two chapters of *Prolégomènes,* and an introductory essay on oral literature requested by Queneau for "Histoire de la littérature universelle" (in *l'Encyclopédie de la Pléiade*).

15 July

I receive a fine letter from Dinu Noica. Speaking of the paralysis of all intellectual activities in Romania, he adds: "I begin to understand that Romanian society has lived and is living by *poussées* [spurts]; the main thing is to preserve ourselves intact for the future. I think how privileged we are to be able to fulfill ourselves through education. And how useful we can be!"

We have lived and are living thus because of geography and our historic destiny. My generation had the great good fortune to develop and begin to create *after 1918*—that is, after the downfall of two imperial systems, the Russian and the German. Twenty years of freedom—that was all we were allowed!

21 July

This afternoon I finish transcribing the study for *Revue d'histoire des religions.* Fifty pages.

* * *

Almost 2:00 A.M., and still I'm in no mood for sleep. Vacation. . . .

For a long time now I've been hearing, when the street becomes quiet, the clatter of a typewriter far off, in another building. Now I've seen where it's coming from: the garret of a house across the way. Someone works there, pecking away with one finger, with great effort. Who can he be, and what is he writing? I look from my room at the little lighted window of the garret, and I can't take my mind off that improbable labor, at 2:00 in the morning, in the maid's chamber.

25 July

I receive, finally, the offprints of "Le Problème du chamanisme." I spend almost the whole day signing and mailing them. Then I write several letters. Again, an SOS to Coomaraswamy, to find me a position, however modest, in an American university.

2 August

After a bad afternoon interrupted by visitors, exhausted from the heat, I begin tonight the chapter on sacred space and write three pages. Without effort but also without brilliance.

7 August

Mediocre days, in which I barely manage to grind out a few pages, poorly written, dull, although the problem of sacred space has intrigued me for years. When I was obliged to work on something else, I would say to myself: How I'd like to be able to write, *now,* the chapter on sacred space for *Prolégomènes!*

8 August

Louis Renou writes me about my competence "*sans égale*" in the field of comparative religions and urges me to persevere and publish. But how? I have nothing left to take to the pawnshop!

9 August

Coomaraswamy replies to the SOS letter I sent him two weeks ago. He has found me a post at a college which is now under

construction and will begin classes in the fall of 1948: the Verde Valley
School, Sedona, Arizona. It is not a university, of course. And I will
teach, at first—French. But in addition to housing, food, electricity,
etc., I will receive twenty-eight hundred dollars per year and will be free
to pursue other interests. Moreover, according to the prospectus he
sends, I would be living in a region of unequaled beauty near the
Colorado River, in the Petrified Forest. I accepted immediately. It's my
only chance to obtain an American visa.

11 August

For three days I've been dreaming of Verde Valley and struggling to finish the chapter on sacred space.

Each "difficult day" yields a meaning only if I look upon my life as
a labyrinthine initiation. (I must decide someday to write all that it
means to go through a labyrinth *without losing one's way.* The meaning
of this initiatory problem has been lost in the Occident ever since the
episode of "Ariadne's thread" was introduced.)

13 August

What a thrill today, while trying to finish the chapter on sacred
space, to discover the nostalgia of archaic man for the lost paradise!
How many things suddenly are made clear to me!

14 August

At Besterman's last night I met again his assistant at UNESCO,
the Swedish Communist sympathizer, a friend of Ziliacus. He says war
is inevitable on account of America's having the atomic bomb, etc.
"What about Russia?" I ask. "Russia makes mistakes out of fear!" he
replies defensively. I see in these few words the slogan of Ziliacus and
the others of the group called "Keep Left." At 11:00 he proposes that
we go to the Tabou. On the way he continues his profession of faith: he
is a Marxist but not a Communist; he believes in honesty, is against the
primacy of the spiritual and the humanism of Léon Blum, opposes A.
Huxley's egotism, etc., etc. But he is almost drunk, and as soon as we
are inside the Tabou he makes his way to the brass rail, orders two

cognacs, and begins to drink alone. The man who believes in honesty, etc.—has forgotten me! I find myself a place at a table and order a lemonade. A quarter of an hour later I signal to him, and he comes and sits beside me in deep silence. A young man with long hair, shirttails out, and wearing sandals approaches me and asks for a hundred francs. "For what?" "So I can go on vacation tomorrow!" I give them to him. The Swede grumbles indignantly, "Vacations, vacations! As though I didn't need a vacation!" Then, without another word, he stands up and goes to the basement, where there is dancing. But upon our arrival the doorkeeper refuses us admission because we aren't "members of the club."

But a few moments later the doorman disappeared. I stayed at my table and waited for my companion to return. I was by no means bored to be alone. The people coming from the lower level, walking unsteadily, were all curious characters: homosexuals, "Existentialists," boys in bathing trunks, girls in slacks (rolled up, as if for yachting), old ladies, South Americans, bearded men, and so on. Everything in that Tabou was strident and artificial, and this fascinated me. "Look at how free and poor we are!" all those young people seemed to be saying, with their sandals, their jackets over their shoulders, and their shirts unbuttoned. "Poor, but artists. . . . And see what an interesting, sophisticated life we lead here in Paris!"

After half an hour the waiter came with the check. My Swedish friend had not returned. I paid—his bill too—and went downstairs to look for him. I found him dancing and terribly drunk. I shook his hand, and he assured me that he'd call me in a day or two so that I could meet the friend of whom we had spoken. Because that was what had brought me to the Tabou—his friend, a Swede, who has lived in France for seven years and is a great expert on Strindberg. He is writing a thesis on Strindberg in Paris. Now, Strindberg has been and remains one of my great passions. . . .

20 August

Following a tedious afternoon and a mediocre film in the evening, I begin, at midnight, the chapter on sacred time, and in less than an hour I write two pages. The subject is one with which I am quite familiar (because it is the central problem in *Archétypes et répétition*), and I am afraid I shall write it rather reluctantly, as it happens whenever I am obliged to repeat, resume, or rewrite things already written.

21 August

I eat with Antoine Bibescu, whom I had not met before, at the Club Union on blvd. de la Madeline (an ultrareactionary club, Antoine informs me). He asks me a thousand things: what I was doing in India, what books I've written in Paris, where I'm publishing them, whom I know, if I've been around the world, etc.

22 August

After a whole day of rain, the heavy curtain of clouds begins to be rent today. Above les Invalides a fragment of heaven reveals itself shyly: a patch of hazy blue far away. It is 11:00 A.M. I have work to do—but it's impossible for me to return to the manuscript, scarcely begun, on magico-religious time. I'm thinking about the fact that I've lived in Paris for almost two years and that I've had to work on things so "foreign" to the locale, instead of being able to return to literature, to read again Balzac, Proust . . . .

24 August

I was awakened a little before dawn by the hooting of screech owls. I've heard them on other nights too, but never were they so shrill or so numerous. There must have been a whole flock of them, and they answered one another with strange, improbable cries.

25 August

I am told, you must be at one with your historical moment. Today we are dominated by the social problem—more precisely, by the social problem as posed by the Marxists. *You must,* therefore, respond through your work, in one way or another, to the historical moment in which you live. . . . Agreed; but I shall try to respond as did the Buddha and Socrates, by transcending their historical moments and *creating* other, new ones or by paving the way for them.

27 August

That which keeps me from living as I should like is the consciousness that I *have* to do something which no one else could do as well as I. It's a paralyzing and humiliating feeling, actually. The ideal that demands fulfillment through me is this: to cease to exist as a living human being in order to limit myself exclusively to the function of producer of "the oeuvre." I recall that Lucian Blaga spoke the same way about himself: that he considered himself simply an "organ," the intermediary through which his philosophical system would come into being and be realized. I don't know what he thinks today about his mission of being "bearer of a system." For me, it becomes at times unendurable. I am not thinking necessarily of the time spent in the preparation and redaction of "the oeuvre." Time is "lost" whatever I do; it is preferable that it be lost in meditating and in writing than at the café. No, it is not about the time devoted to "the oeuvre" that I lament but about my lost liberty. How many other freedoms would I not allow myself, if I didn't feel bound by the books I *haven't* written!

28 August

Toward morning I dreamed that I'd become a Balzac enthusiast again, and I was in the bookstore on rue Bonaparte. I've stopped in front of that store a number of times to admire the volumes by and about Balzac that are displayed in the window. Then I regretted—and yet, at the same time, I congratulated myself, because what could I do about it in my poverty?—that I am no longer so devoted to Balzac as I once was, that I don't suffer insomnia at the thought of being unable to procure a certain book of unpublished materials, correspondence, etc. In my dream, I conversed with the proprietress of the bookstore concerning Bardèche's book, about which she had spoken to me once (when I visited the store with Besterman for a Voltaire item). I woke up with a crazy urge to reread *La Cousine Bette* and with memories of Mihail Sebastian, in whom I tried for so many years to instill a passion for Balzac and who, I had heard, became a "Balzacian" in the last years of his life.

29 August

I resume work on the chapter about sacred time, but toward evening discouragement gets the better of me. I'm thinking about the fact that summer has passed and that still I have not received the proofs from Gallimard. When will *Prolégomènes* ever appear? Where and when will I publish *Archétypes et répétition?* Depressed, I go for a stroll on the quays. I search for a book by Balzac, and I find *Le Cousin Pons,* the Garnier edition (prefaced and annotated by Maurice Allen). Tonight I begin reading it. Fortunately, I remembered it rather well (fortunately, because otherwise I'd have abandoned *Prolégomènes* again).

It's strange, however, that this sudden inclination to reread Balzac is due to yesterday's dream.

31 August

Am progressing slowly in *Le Cousin Pons.* It would be extremely interesting to see, from the galley proofs and manuscripts, how Balzac worked out this novel, how he transformed the novella of which Mme. Hanska spoke into a rather lengthy novel. A series of additions are transparent: for example, chapter 32, "Traité des sciences occultes," and probably the chapter immediately following with "le grand jeu" and the description of the house of Elias Magus. I wonder what the novel would have become if it had kept the proportions planned by Balzac at the outset. As it is, it begins to obsess you once Pons is thrown out by Mme. Camusot. You can't put it down after that.

Reading chapter 32, I remembered my lecture at the Dalles Foundation when I spoke of Balzac as mystic and visionary. Actually, I limited myself then mainly to *Séraphita* and to the Swedenborgian elements in his works. But it would be interesting to take up the problem again as a whole. (Probably this project will become one of the numerous books I shall never write!)

* * *

I've been thinking of starting a special notebook for recording facts, impressions, quotations. But I say to myself that such a notebook, cut off from the horizon of my current concerns, would be in danger of becoming a lifeless dossier. I prefer to record here, even if only in a haphazard way, some of these impressions of my readings. It will amuse me someday to reread them, along with the occasional notes on Balzac in my journal for 1933–40.

* * *

Reread in 1947 after all I've known in the past several years, *Le Cousin Pons* fascinates me for the authenticity of its monsters. Only recently have I *seen* what ambition, human passion, intrigue, parvenuism, and the desire to reach the top at any price really mean. When I read Balzac in adolescence and youth, these pages seemed to be mere "literature"; they fascinated me because they succeeded in obsessing me—but I didn't *believe* in those people. Now that I've known them in real life, Balzac's perspicacity makes me shiver. How profoundly and precisely has he seen the society of the nineteenth century, sick with cupidity, dominated by a thirst for power, by ambition, and by the desire to "arrive" socially and politically! The hell out of which the new ranks of bourgeoisie are constantly arising.

2 September

I think sometimes about writing a book that will express me *entirely.* I'd withdraw for several weeks into an isolated place—an island, a cabin on a mountaintop (the ideal spot would be Tierra del Fuego!), without any books or manuscripts. With nature presenting no interest, I'd begin to recall my life—in order to "populate" that wilderness. I'd write a kind of journal, but without an order of any sort. Memories, reflections, commentaries on my own thoughts, my books, etc. In that perfect solitude, in that forlorn landscape, I'd try to reveal myself wholly, with all my passions: literature, philosophy, history of religions, orientalistics, mysticism, adventure.

4 September

Last night, being unable to work any longer at the chapter on scared time, I read *Le Père Goriot* until almost 3:00 A.M. I believe this is my eighth or ninth reading of that formidable novel (my favorite, as a "realistic" novel, out of Balzac's whole oeuvre). I recall the first time

I read it at age ten. Several years later I reread it right after finishing *Gobseck*. On that day (in 1919 or 1920) I became a ''Balzacian'': I had discovered how the characters in *La Comédie humaine* are interrelated. Then, with my classmate Marculescu, a recent convert to Balzac, I began to comb the used bookstores. There was almost nothing to be found. (What joy when one of use chanced upon *Le Centenaire*!) We even had plans for the two of us to translate the entire Balzac corpus. I believe I started a translation of *Louis Lambert*. This enthusiasm lasted all through lycée. A second great Balzacian period was 1934–37. I read then his whole oeuvre. Or, rather, I reread it. In a single summer I read *La Père Goriot* twice. . . . What pleasure it gives me to be able *now* to identify Parisian landscapes! What a thrill to discover that Gobseck had his shop on the present rue Cujas!

* * *

I've given myself a few days' leave from *Prolégomènes*. I read without stopping *Les Débuts littéraires d'Honoré de Balzac* by L. J. Arrigon and have begun *Les Années romantiques de Balzac* by the same author. My passion for minute, *concrete* details is amply satisfied.

5 September

I finish *Les Années romantiques de Balzac* and *Le Père Goriot* today. I believe that in the past two days I've read Balzac for more than thirty-two hours, driven by a fever that reminds me of my adolescence. It's 1:00 A.M., and I have nothing more to read. I can't do anything else; I can't read any other book.

In 1821 Balzac wrote to his sister Laure: ''. . . je n'ai que deux passions: l'amour et la gloire, et rien n'est encore satisfait, rien ne le sera jamais''* [I have but two passions: love and glory, and neither is yet satisfied, nor ever will be]. Balzac's awkward debuts! His lack of culture, taste, and talent; his terrible conceitedness! The influence of his contemporaries, of the taste and fashions of the time. He writes what is being written, what is being read. And yet, little by little, he finds

---

*Text incorrect; for the exact reading, see Hastings's edition.

himself and becomes the titan without peer. Then follows that conquest of self, which to me seems more remarkable than even his genius.

The first truly Balzacian work was badly received by the critics. In contrast, when he was still groping around and writing grotesque and fantastic novels which he did not sign, he sometimes had the good luck to be appreciated. "*Le Pilote* publia un article très élogieux sur la *Dernière Fée* qu'il comparait au *Diable amoureux* de Cazotte et au *Mari Sylphe* de Marmontel" [*Le Pilote* publishes a very flattering article about *Dernière Fée,* comparing it to Cazotte's *Diable amoureux* and Marmontel's *Mari Sylphe*] (*Les débuts littéraires,* p. 152).

6 September

La Maison Nucingen, which I had read only once and without being won over by it, has failed to captivate me this time also. Written in November 1837, it mentions Stendhal: "un des hommes les plus spirituels et les plus profonds de cette époque . . ." [one of the most witty and most profound men of that era]. And two reflections of the Blondet wit: "Tout homme supérieur doit avoir, sur les femmes, les opinions de l'Orient . . ." [Every superior man ought to have, concerning women, Oriental opinions]; "L'amour est la seule chance qu'aient les sots pour grandir" [Love is the only chance fools have for growth].

7 September

La Maison de Balzac, at 47 rue Raynouard, Passy. I thought I'd find a true Balzac museum, with manuscripts, objects, and books. A single autograph: the letter by which he informed the publisher of the plan of *La Comédie humaine.* Many paintings and portraits, most of them reproductions. A large number of busts, a mock-up of the fresco, "La Comédie humaine," from 1901: second-rate and not really Balzacian. His coffeepot and his inkwell. His workroom. (The furniture was sold by creditors.) Balzac's hand. The guard pointed out to me how shrunken it was. "He began to decompose very quickly. They were scarcely able to get a plaster mold of it. And they say that no one could stay very long in the mortuary room."

His garden, with a view over the Seine. Opposite, a palace Balzac hoped to buy for two hundred thousand francs. Today it is occupied by the Turkish legation. In the garden, a little vine in the rear; elder, wild roses. It gives the impression of an abandoned property. Balzac lived here in Passy between 1840 and 1846, his most creative years. Here he lived the hell of eighteen-hour working days. And I saw the trapdoor through which he fled into a passageway under the garden when his creditors came looking for him!

When I arrived at 2:30 there was only one other visitor: an elderly American woman who was resting on a bench in the garden and smiling. Presently she asked the guard whether he had a visitors' register, and she began to turn the pages. She found Joffre, P. Bourget, and Zweig. However, she was looking for the name of a certain great American Balzac fan, but she never did find it.

* * *

"Elle pensa que les hommes de génie devaient aimer avec beaucoup plus de perfection que n'aiment les fats, les gens du monde, les diplomates et même les militaires, que cependant n'ont que cela à faire" [She thought that men of genius ought to love with much greater perfection than dandies, men of the world, diplomats, and even soldiers, who have nothing else to do] (*Les Secrets de la princesse de Cadignan*). She makes this reflection after the writer d'Arthez kisses her "avec une si délicate volupté, que la princesse inclina la tête en augurant très bien de la littérature" [with such a delicate voluptuousness that the princess bowed her head, auguring very favorably for literature]. Balzacian autobiography.

8 September

I return to *Prolégomènes* and write five pages, almost finishing the chapter on sacred time.

This evening I begin reading *Honorine*. "Il cultivait Dieu comme certaines honnêtes gens cultivent un vice, avec in profond mystère" [He cultivates God as certain honest people cultivate a vice: with a mystery].

11 September

Barbul, who arrived here from Romania on 5 August, seeks me out this morning. All he tells me about the terror in the homeland depresses me and at the same time hardens and embitters me.

16 September

Perhaps, after all, I shall write someday a long essay about Balzac. With that in mind, while rereading *La Peau de chagrin,* I began taking notes on loose sheets of paper. Am also reading *Les Orientations étrangères chez Honoré de Balzac* and a simple doctoral thesis, *Balzac et le monde slave,* which seems almost insipid beside the marvelous Baldensperger.

20 September

G. Tucci writes me that he is leaving for Tibet in January. He is in perfect accord with all I have written about shamanism. A number of works on Bon-po, in the press or in preparation, confirm me, he says.

21 September

In the past few days I've been reading Balzac exclusively (the first volume of his correspondence was a revelation!). I've filled several copybooks with notes and extracts.

23 September

I venture inside the Georges Courville bookstore, 88 rue Bonaparte, for the first time today. The proprietress greets me and, on learning that I am a historian of religions and an orientalist, she begins telling me about her "spiritualistic" experiences on the "mental plane." She is about fifty, stout, with a Kalmuk face. Her cheeks were glowing today because, as she hastened to inform me, apologetically, she is undergoing treatment with penicillin ("externally, of course"). She is a very good "medium," she tells me. She heals people at a distance, simply by concentration. Once she concentrates, she passes onto "another plane." She is "guided" directly. She has not had masters, but she had an illness. This occurred in India, where, as a practicing Catholic, she lost her faith and contracted a grave psychosis. Also, she had a "revelation of a sentence of Vivekananda" (?!); she said that the first sentence he addressed to her was the one she had heard in India. . . . And a great many other things of the same caliber, to which I listened with a smile on my lips, expressing approval as often as I could—because she had told me she can show her Balzac collections to "reliable persons" and even permit them to work in a room in the back of her store.

28 September

After three days of cold weather—suddenly the light of autumn. On the quays this morning. The smoky haze of Paris is gone, and instead only the gentle warmth of a heaven so blue it astonishes you. One would have expected it to be yellowish.

I've been working fifteen to sixteen hours per day, and I have exhausted the essential documents, both at home and at the library, about the college at Vendôme and Balzac's adolescence. Yesterday I sketched that sad and pathetic adolescence in five pages. Today, in spite of the beauty that entices me to the window, I had planned to work on those pages and make a nearly definitive text. I don't know how much more time I'll have free to spend on my Balzacian passion. It would be a shame to waste so much enthusiasm and so much work.

29 September

And yet I'm afraid to let myself be drawn into this adventure. First I must finish *Prolégomènes* and the other studies already begun. But I shall continue my Balzacian readings, and I shall prepare the documentation—for later.

1 October

Have been to see Jamati, director of le Centre de la recherche scientifique. I found out that he has accorded me an "aide de savant" of twenty-five thousand francs, which I will receive shortly. As for the monthly allotment I had requested—it will be examined in October.

(The truth is, in the June session the request was rejected, or maybe—I hope!—only postponed, "for political reasons.") At any rate, the twenty-five thousand francs will rescue me from many difficulties.

11 October

Festy, the director of *"fabrication"* at Gallimard writes me that *Techniques du Yoga* has been held up until now because the printers they have engaged don't have the diacritical signs required. And because of these "signs," for which italics could very well have been substituted, I have lost a year!

12 October

Went to see Masson-Oursel today to ask him to recommend me to le Centre de la recherche scientifique. We spoke, among other things, about Dasgupta. His second wife, a very young woman it seems, has enrolled for doctoral studies at the Sorbonne. Everyone is very curious to meet her. Masson-Oursel adds: "It seems she took care of him during an illness. That's why he married her. If she saved his life, she deserves every honor!"

13 October

All night I was obsessed by the "revelations" made by Octave Mirbeau about Balzac's final agony and death. But still I hesitate to believe them. It would be necessary to see the whole file. In any event, even if invented, these "revelations" constitute the most Balzacian death the author of *La Comedie humaine* could have had.

Puech tells me that he will be the one to report on my request at le Centre de recherche scientifique. That's good news!

21 October

What have I done in all these glorious and incredible days of autumn? Balzacian euphoria, visits to insure my getting the grant from le Centre de recherche scientifique, walks in a Paris congested and in a state of unrest on account of a strike of metro and bus drivers. I see the Bonnard exposition at Orangerie. Only a few canvases please me: still lives and flowers in which white, yellow, and orange predominate. I continue to write (mainly for my own enjoyment) the biographical essay on Balzac. Have reached the years 1819–20, at the garret on rue Lesdiguières. I am happy to be able to know so well the "neighborhood" and to know it on this kind of autumn, hot and protracted—one could say, precisely like the autumn of 1819, when Honoré discovered his freedom.

This evening, a Chopin recital with Dinu Lipatti at Champs-Elysées. The "Finale" from the Sonata op. 58 in B Minor, reminded me, suddenly, of 1922–23 when I deciphered that haunting melody and whistled it for my fellow lycée pupils during recess time.

22 October

Puech gives me the good news that I have been proposed for the post of *maître de recherchès* at about 250,000 francs per annum.

27 October

A young man, Negust, comes to see me. He has a quixotic face, a large nose, black curly hair—and the voice of a cantor, which seems so incongruous when you first hear it that you listen with a smile until he convinces you that it is his natural voice. He is a sculptor of sorts, but he is preoccupied above all with religious problems. That is, he reads the New Testament—one of the four books he declares he has read in his lifetime. I believe that the fourth was *Insula lui Euthanasius;* this is what prompted him to come to see me. (Something to do with Parsifal and "universal myths"—in distinction, he says, from the *Miorița,* which is a "local myth.") For two years he attended classes at Academia Comercială in Bucharest, failing both years. He spent four months cutting paper (yes, from morning to night, cutting newspapers, with a pair of scissors, into narrower and narrower strips! Nervous, he found nothing calmed him except to have newspapers in front of him and scissors in hand. And since he tells me that at about the same time he wanted to kill his parents, I think what an exciting subject for a psychoanalyst this mania for cutting up newspapers would be!) He loafed around almost all this time, without friends, without feeling any need to read. Two and a half years ago he came clandestinely to Paris. But he still can speak no French because he knows no one. He has lived by painting, sleeping at friends' places. Currently, he is staying at Fontenay-aux-Roses. He associates mainly with the children of the former Romanian consul in Paris, Constantinescu: a boy of eighteen and a girl of seventeen. The latter he is in love with and hopes to marry—after she has "risen to his level."

9 November

Learning from her nephew, Andrei Costin, that I am in Paris, Maruca Cantacuzino Enesco invites me today to her place in Bellevue. She had sent word already that she has wanted for twelve years to meet me, and she repeats this as soon as I enter the house. Somewhat excited, I climb the stairs of this villa, sad at the onset of sunset. Many trees, dampness, the smell of fallen leaves. How well all these melancholy things fitted in with all that followed! Because Maruca begins at once to talk about Nae [Ionescu]. She asks me whether I remember the Villa of Pines in Şosea. How could I not! But this past is no longer haunting or depressing for her. At sixty-eight (she looks hardly fifty-eight), memories no longer hurt the way they do at twenty or forty. I see that she is still happy that all these things had happened to *her,* that she had known Nae and had loved him. Just once, recalling I don't know what gesture, I caught her moved almost to the point of tears.

Unfortunately, a number of other guests were present, and we weren't able to talk very much about Nae. There ensued the inevitable general discussion about mysticism, religion, occultism, ecstasy—and Ana Pauker, plus the disasters in our homeland. Maruca speaks in capital letters: the Absolute, Life, Ideal. Of course, she is by no means silly or commonplace. An observing spirit, surprising expressions. And the thing that fascinates me: the vanity of a woman who wants at all costs to remain superior, surrounding herself exclusively with superior people, directing conversations toward "the heights." I can see her very well in a drawing room, holding sway over a capital, changing governments, naming ministers. Nae's fall, it seems, stemmed from the misunderstanding and hostility between Maruca and the Lupescu woman.

As I am leaving, she gives me two typed manuscripts, one of which, called "Silhouette," bears the dedication: "A Mr. M. Eliade, Abîmes . . . et Flamme" [To M. E., Abysses . . . and Flames]. It is a portrait of Nae—and it's not at all bad. It emphasizes Nae's demonism, his terror regarding nonbeing, his nihilism. She confesses that she often saw in him the devil, and that only in the first two years of "notre éthérique compagnonnage dans le domaine de l'Esprit et l'exaltation metaphysique" had Nae Ionescu known a relative unity of his being. Although, she adds, at the end, during the last two years he lived, Nae's life was brightened by one of the most intelligent and seductive women he had ever known, i.e., Cella Delavranca.

At the foot of the stairs, as I am leaving, I meet the Maestro, to whom Maruca introduces me. He is much more stooped and decrepit than I had imagined him. And in spite of this, he travels all over France, giving concerts every day, he sleeps only four hours per night, and writes all the time.

Andrei Costin informs me on the way home that Maruca had asked him how she might be of help to me and whether I were in need of money. I reply that I am grateful but that I hope to be able to manage alone.

15 November

Dinner at Bellevue. Maruca Cantacuzino Enesco reads me the act of donation conveying her estate and house at Teşcani to the Romanian government. Then she shows me the letter she sent to the administrator of the estate, to explain to the villagers why she had made the donation. The letter moved me by virtue of all the melancholies it awakened. The administrator had received it, had read it to the villagers—and three days later he had died, suddenly, in his bed.

19 November

For the first time in some two months, I stop work today on the Balzac essay in order to correct the typewritten copy of the three chapters of *Prolégomènes,* worked on and translated this summer. The folder had lain waiting on my table for several weeks, but as usual when I'm caught up in a task, I can't do anything else.

28 November

In these past several days when I've interrupted work on the Balzac essay in order to write several studies in the history of religions which had been postponed for so many days—and in these days of transition from fall to winter (even as I write, snow has begun to fall)—I have lived in a state of continual alteration. First I would see *ahead* of me the numerous projected works and the exhilarating prospects; then I would look only *backward* and would see my life thus far as a series of failures and disasters, and I would be conscious of all I *have not done* and *have not experienced* in the past twenty years. This "attack" would come over me at least once a day. And then, almost abruptly, I would awake on another "horizon" where the forty years I have had, the "history" I sense behind me, played no role, almost as though they *didn't exist.* On the contrary, I would feel that only the *time from now on* becomes worthy of being known; only from now on does existing in time begin to mean something worthwhile and, more particularly, begin to have a theoretical validity. (These things are much more complex than I'm attempting to describe them here. I'll have to return to them someday.)

30 November

At Georges Enesco's home for dinner. The maestro seems less tired and less bent than last time. Small talk during the mealtime. Then, over coffee in the drawing room which was still frigid (although I myself had kindled a fire when I came), with his legs stretched out on a footstool and with Mutzi, the cat, in his arms, he allowed himself a few puns and jokes. When a meal is digesting, he says, he doesn't like to be "transcendent." In fact, like any man who works and creates, he likes to relax "in the world." He evokes the Paris of 1910 and speaks of Vaschide, who killed himself trying to be a scholar and a man of the world at the same time, sleeping only three hours per night.

I believe that the maestro, and Maruca as well, are in rather modest circumstances. His numerous concerts are given only for the money, because, as he confesses to me, he can't stand being on the road and would rather stay at home as much as possible to work, write, etc

3 December

Another bolt of lightning has struck when I was no longer expecting it. The director of le Centre de la recherche scientifique informs me that my request has not been approved!

4 December

Puech doesn't understand what's happened. I was second on the list! He will speak with Le Bras, who is a member of the directorate, and if Le Bras won't give me satisfaction, Puech will resign from the commission. He does not understand what purpose their advice serves, if the directorate decides as it pleases.

Dumézil is indignant. He assures me that there must be some political intrigue back of it. He is awaiting the return of Lucien Febvre from Mexico in order to find out what is the matter, to see whether something can be done.

I, on the contrary, am entertaining no illusions.* I know that this, too, is a part of my destiny.

6 December

. . . And yet I'm not depressed. I don't know why, but the last blow received, that from le Centre de la recherche scientifique, hardens me. The resistance I sense increasing around me and in front of me begins to flatter me. I ought to write more about this invigorating sensation I've been experiencing for the past few days, but it's been so long since I abandoned the habit of writing a proper journal that I don't feel disposed to review the matter now. As I turn the pages of this notebook, I realize how badly it betrays me. I find here almost nothing of what the autumn of 1947 really has meant for me: neither the myth of the Romanian diaspora which gives meaning to my exiled existence, nor my conception of biography (occasioned by the essay about Balzac on which I'm currently working), nor the important discoveries I've made concerning "primitive" religions (from my studies of the Dyaks of Borneo).

*I was not mistaken. It was impossible to do anything [author's note].

9 December

Puech tells me Lucien Febvre and G. Le Bras have in mind to protest vigorously to the directorate about the intervention of the police (because, as it turns out, this was the case: the Romanian police intervened to prevent my being granted a stipend for study).

I go to Payot to show him the manuscript of *Prolégomènes*. I'll have the result in a few days.

11 December

Payot telephoned twice this morning, first to summon me urgently to the publishing house (immediately, if possible!) and the second time to ask me in how many days I can have the manuscript finished, because he has a printer available in Paris.

I see him at 4:00 this afternoon. The book is engaged; it will appear in the spring (but I still have two chapters to write!). If I deliver the manuscript to him in eight days, we will sign the contract and I will receive an advance of sixty thousand francs. I think I'm dreaming! And this book, which I've been carrying around for eight years, on which I've been working for almost four, so many times begun and laid aside—will have to be finished in a few weeks.

13 December

I worked all day yesterday and all night until 6:00 A.M. (as in the good old days of my youth!). Upon awakening I find the letter with the contract from Payot: when I hand over the manuscript I will be paid the sum of seventy-five thousand francs! It seems fabulous.

I am writing these lines toward 4:00 A.M. The correcting of the manuscript and the final touches to the bibliography are going rather slowly.

18 December

I looked at the calendar to see what day it is. For a week I've been working like a madman, every night till 6:00 A.M. Since I wake up, whether I want to or not, between 11:00 and 12:00, I'm about twenty hours deficient in sleep. But today, finally, I finished revising the manuscript, with the bibliographies, titles, subtitles, etc. I took it to Payot, and he handed me a check for seventy-five thousand francs. He asked me to provide the rest in fifteen days—that is, the preface, a foreword by Dumézil, and the two final chapters (which, of course, I avoided saying weren't written yet). And so, a day of rest, and then I begin again.

30 December

Bad luck! For five days I've been wrestling with a new bout of vagotonia. I can work only with a tremendous effort—a few poor pages a day. I've written just twelve of the sixty I must present, typed and corrected, to Dumézil on 15 January.

1 January 1948

I feel that the vagotonia has left me. The first day without any pain or drowsiness. I must make up for lost time, prudently and without too great an effort.

10 January

Although I still have to write the last chapter on symbolism, I spent the whole day and night reading Balzac, going from *Contes drolatiques* to *L'Enfant maudit*. This too, is a part of the paradox of my existence, and I must resign myself to it.

24 January

I finish, finally, the last chapter of *Prolégomènes*.

10 February

With mounting fascination I reread *La Fille aux yeux d'or*, definitely one of the most beautiful creations of the youthful Balzac. His description of Parisian "circles"—in the Dantean sense of the term— seems to me, at this date, simply marvelous. How splendid for Balzac was the mission of the writer!

There are so many lines I'd like to copy out. I abandon the idea. "Bientôt fatigués de donner sans recevoir, ils (les quelques hommes

valides) restent chez eux et laissent régner les sots sur leur terrain''
[Soon fatigued by giving without receiving, they (the healthy men)
remain in their places and let fools rule on their terrain].

13 February

A number of reflections on the Romanian diaspora. So many
problems arise in connection with our spiritual development. The
inevitable dramas, linked to the very condition of ''political emigration,'' are in danger of sterilizing us and dissipating us. What measures
can we take to maintain ourselves ''alive, healthy, and creative?'' (Who
used that expression?)

14 February

Hamilton writes me from the Verde Valley School that, not
having the opportunity to meet me and know me personally (because he
has abandoned his plans for a trip to Europe), he cannot hire me, for the
time being, as a teacher. Therefore, yet another illusion. . . .

18 February

I receive the proofs of *Techniques du Yoga*. The text was finished
two years ago, but there are also pages in it taken from my doctoral
thesis which I wrote *in 1930* in Calcutta!

25 February

I haven't written anything in this notebook for some time, being
exhausted both from my ailments (somnolence, migraines, flu) and
from numerous visits and discussions. I've revised and sent off the
proofs of the study for *Revue de l'histoire des religions*, ''Le 'Dieu lier'
et le symbolisme des noeuds.'' At last, a text that does not disappoint
me when I reread it!

26 February

At the Collège Philosophique, Georges Bataille speaks about
. . . the history of religions. After making some observations during
the discussion period, I meet him and we talk a little while. He invites

me to contribute to *Critique*. He sets a date to come and see me next week.

4 March

Georges Bataille comes today. He asks me to write a book on Tantrism, which he would publish immediately. In fact, the hour we spent together was largely "confiscated" by Tantrism. He told me that after a three-years' search of the Bibliothèque Nationale where he was a functionary, he was surprised to discover that the most lucid exposition of Tantrism was in a book published in Bucharest (my *Yoga* of 1936).

5 March

The Romanian diaspora—the extension and amplification of the transhumance of Romanian pastoralism. The role of pastoral nomadism in Romanian folk-spirituality, the opposition to the "closed world" of the sedentary ploughmen. *Dor* [longing, nostalgia], the "Miorița" and so many other famous ballads—the creation of that nomadism. Someday someone will make precise the tension between the diaspora (emigration) and the zealots (staying power). We must know how to defend ourselves from a neo-chauvinistic provincialism. . . .

* * *

The extreme specialization of the sciences in the nineteenth century coincides with the birth and triumph of nationalism and the nation-state. Imperial conceptions and "federal" systems correspond to global spiritual visions. The world of tomorrow: "federalism" and empires. The models: Leonardo, Leibniz, Goethe.

12 March

I go to Payot to inquire when I will receive the proofs. And I learn that, because of a tremendous increase in the price of paper and type, the publishing house has withdrawn all manuscripts. I shall have to wait another three months, or perhaps six. . . .

* * *

Invited for dinner this evening by Prince Raymond of Thurn and Taxis, the present owner of the castle at Duino. (I met him through Jean

Gouillard.) A likable young fellow, speaking the five aristocratic languages of Europe with equal facility and yet with affectation and an uncertain accent. He has been all over the world, and he travels constantly. He arrived here a few days ago from London, and he leaves next week for Italy. He will be a "guest" also at Duino, currently occupied by the British. Then, because he has a hankering for Sweden, he will go there. Earlier he visited Fatehpur-Sikhri, Fiji (where he witnessed a ritual of walking on hot coals), Japan. . . . We talked about oriental religions and yoga, because it was for this reason he wanted to meet me: to find out how one can become a yogin without having to live in Himalaya.

After dinner the prince shows me photos of the castle. Here, on this promenade, Rilke had the inspiration for his first elegy, etc. There follow the inevitable ghost stories. The painter, Lou Lasarus, arrives; she went to India in 1937 with Lanza del Vasto and resided for several weeks at Rishikesh. She has made an excellent translation of the "Duinese Elegies," and she recites them with great sensitivity. Recollections and observations about Rilke: his ambivalent tendencies toward solitude and companionship, the feeling that he had made a failure of his life, his passion for women, etc. He was quickly aroused by every woman he met, and to each he repeated the same things. About his legitimate daughter he would say: "Qu'est-ce qu'il me fait cet objet hollandais?"

13 March

In a discussion at Lizica Codreanu's place last night, I propose to several psychoanalysts present a parallel interpretation, in cosmological and metaphysical terms, of infantile eroticism. For example, the attraction of the boy for his mother and of the girl for her father corresponds in mythology and cosmology to the *tendance* of the Spirit toward "matter" and to the attraction of "matter" for spirit. Of course, the male infant can be homologized to a phallus trying to reintegrate itself into the maternal womb, but he *must* likewise be compared to the Spirit's tendency to be reintegrated in the Primordial Substance, thereby restoring the unity of *esse-non esse* from before creation. Infantile sexuality must be interpreted also within the perspective revealed by the symbolism of the Androgyne, present—and active—in every human being. Separated from the maternal womb, the infant male seeks to recover the prenatal unity, a sort of larval androgyny. The girl, on the other hand, feels attracted to that which she was not, even in the maternal uterus, but what she was *first,* only in the moment of conception. . . .

15 March

Human behavior seen in an organic perspective: there are certain people who behave in life as a stomach, others as a liver, others as a sex organ, a brain, etc. It is notable how many persons conduct themselves as minor or obscure organs, such as an appendix or a nose.

10 April

Yesterday evening, at le Centre de recherches spirituelles, a public discussion with Paul Masson-Oursel on Indian mysticism.

This morning, along with the proofs of the article for *Critique* which I had sent him two weeks ago, I receive a letter from Georges Bataille informing me that I can start immediately on the book on Tantrism. . . . But I have so many things to finish before I can devote myself to Tantrism! Above all, the lectures for l'Ecole des hautes études which I keep postponing.

22 April

The first lecture on "Techniques du yoga" at le Centre des recherches spirituelles, in a small assembly hall back of Vibade's bookstore, 13 rue de l'Odéon. Many ladies "of a certain age," devotees of "the Spirit," India, occultism, etc., plus a few psychoanalysts from Dr. Winter's circle.

Amusing intrusion: Prince Galitzin, with his elongated face and thick, black, drooping mustache, looking like a character out of Eça de Quéiroz.

29 April

The second lecture at le Centre des recherches spirituelles. Among those who take part in the discussion I notice—with considerable apprehension at first—a police sergeant, a cop with beautiful blue eyes. It is he, in fact, who asks the most interesting questions regarding the annihilation of the ego in Buddhism.

3 May

I receive this morning the first copy of *Techniques du Yoga*. The appearance of this book doesn't make me as happy as I had expected. It comes too late. . . . How glad I'd be if I knew that *Prolégomènes* would appear soon!

13 May

I see the documentary film, *1900* (comprising excerpts taken from seven hundred movies of that era!). What ugly people, and how distant seems to me that "paradisiacal" age from which we are separated by only forty or fifty years! Scenes from the Comédie-française, although they were played by the leading actors of the time, are simply grotesque. Only D'Annunzio's greyhounds and the Parisian monuments are not "dated." After all the bearded men and corseted women, only those few agile and impatient greyhounds look natural, only they remain unmodified by "history." I don't think it's a matter only of clothing, beards, and imperfections of film and cameras. People of 1900 were "dated" even by their behavior, their philosophy, their delights. We can no longer make use of anything from their *life,* although we can learn much from the life of a Romantic poet or an author of the seventeenth century or a Greek of the Golden Age.

24 May

Am surprised and delighted at such a positive reaction from the first readers of *Techniques du Yoga* (Puech, Gaston Bachelard, etc.). Louis Renou writes me: "Dans la masse de littérature insipide ou fausse relative au Yoga, vous avez réussi le *premier* à écrire un livre exact, bien documenté, vigoureusement pensé" [In the mass of insipid or false literature relative to Yoga, you are the *first* to have succeeded in writing a book that is correct, well documented, and vigorously thought out]. I copy these few lines as a gentle reprimand addressed to the lamentations with which I covered so many pages here while writing the book.

26 May

At Vera Daumal's. She tells me about her husband and his marvelous efforts to achieve an "interior" life. He separated from Leconte when the latter, wanting to go to the extreme limits of experience, let himself become addicted to drugs. René Daumal himself took drugs at eighteen, in order to obtain a "supraprofane experience." But he stopped doing it overnight when he observed that they beclouded other sectors of his consciousness.

Vera Daumal showed me his notebooks with translations from Sanskrit, and that extraordinary grammar which René constructed by himself. With the aid of this grammar, she said, a friend learned Sanskrit in three months (!).

27 May

I begin, finally, the series of lectures at l'Ecole des hautes études on "The Structure of Myths." Afterward, several persons come to talk with me. A lady approaches with a package in her hand: it contains the works of Marie de Naglowska on sexuality, *La Lumière du sexe, Le Mystère de la pendaison,* and a collection of the magazine, *La Flèche.* The lady begs me insistently to take great care with them, to hide them in my closet under lock and key, because they are "very dangerous initiatory texts," etc. Leafing through them at home, I am depressed by their absolute vacuity.

10 June

. . . . Tonight I stand for a long time at the window, gazing into the darkness, listening to the rustling of the trees in the yard next door. It has become almost cold, after two days of sudden, intense heat. I can breathe; I find myself again, I can think. Goethe comes to mind once more: I think of the miracle of his existence, of the "burden of history" he never had to suffer. To be able to live integrally, without letting yourself live in "time," to live only in the instant and not let yourself be poisoned or crushed by the past, by "history" . . . .

15 June

At l'Arc-en-Ciel, Aimé Patri speaks about Malcolm de Chazal, and André Breton reads selections from *Sens plastique*. Upon my being introduced to Breton (an exceptionally gentle and modest man, of a noble beauty, though looking a bit weary), I listen to the most surprising "compliments." At the end of the lecture, a long discussion about the nature of the suprasensible and poetic experiences of Chazal.

26 June

Last night, at Dr. Hunwald's, with M. and Mme. André Breton, Péret, and Aimé Patri also present. The discussion drifts to alchemy and magic. Although he is willing to utilize them as sources of poetic inspiration, Breton does not believe in the "reality" of paranormal phenomena or occult techniques. For the author of such a text as "Sur le peu de réalité," this attitude is baffling and bizarre. But I suspect that Breton is staging a performance with his new Cartesian and "positivistic" attitude, when, for instance, he denies stigmata, even those of a hysterical nature, on the grounds that "hysteria does not exist as an autonomous reality" but was cultivated and promoted at Salpetrière, etc. Breton is frightened at the attempts of a few "spiritualists" to incorporate his message. Claude Mauriac is preparing a book, *Saint André Breton,* and he sent him at Christmas a card with a crucifix on it. . . . Breton defends himself by pretending to be happy to have rediscovered "matter."

5 July

Georges Bataille, just back from England, comes to see me, and we talk for two hours. This time we succeed in having a more coherent conversation, helping each other to see problems and solutions more clearly. . . . I shall record here only one detail. Speaking about the need for "orgies," he told me this experience: he is invited to a mediocre apartment, furnished in glaringly bad taste, where there are gathered some bourgeois types: tight, nervous (since they know what is to follow!), looking at the paintings on the walls, making critical observations, etc. A strained atmosphere: anxiety, tension. A drinking bout follows and eventually an "orgy." As if by miracle, these insipid, artificial, shriveled, vacuous people stop being "themselves" and become brilliant, alive—persons of a noble and quite unexpected *presence*. The regression into an "orgy," by abolishing their petit-bourgeois categories, regenerated them and restored in them a human presence.

Interesting observations by Bataille about the anxiety that precedes the "orgy," the last resistance of "being" to the "non-being" that is to follow. An anxiety which is found preliminary to every profound and authentic religious experience.

20 August

For some time now I've been filling in for a Belgian functionary at UNESCO (a temporary position, arranged by Besterman). I have come to understand finally why, despite all their good intentions, men who have a "job" can scarcely do anything else—at least after a certain age.

29 August

We are greeted by the sun of Marseilles, after a sleepless night in a third-class railway coach—Giza, Martha Voiculescu, and I. In the station, the IRO refugees stand in line, filling a large share of the platform.

We look for a hotel. The girls find themselves a room at Hôtel Nice-Paris, the last one available. I content myself with a basement cubicle requiring artificial lights at all times. The manager informs me that it had been an air-raid shelter. We eat at the port amid the shouts, cries, and songs of the sailors who are trying to attract passengers for Chateau d'If.

This afternoon we take the cable car up to Notre Dame de la Garde. In the chapel all sorts of souvenirs and fetish objects are for sale. "Non, pour les aviateurs nous n'avons rein pour l'instant!" said the nun to the sad girl beside her.

We descent to the port on foot.

30 August

To Hôtel Saint-Louis to find out the time when the IRO bus comes to take the passengers to the dock. At 12:30 Giza boards the bus; we aren't allowed to go with her. It takes us two hours to obtain a laissez-passer. We reach the dock at 4:00. The *Campana* is an enormous ocean liner. Almost a thousand immigrants for Argentina are waiting in line to embark. Giza is courageous. After going aboard, she calls to us several times from the deck: "When will we see one another again?" Soon the whistle sounds, and the *Campana* departs slowly from the dock. For a long time we can distinguish clearly her green dress in that crowd massed on the deck, waving handkerchiefs.

8 September

I receive today the first batch of proof of *Prolégomènes,* the title of which will be, at Payot's insistence, *Traité d'histoire des religions.* I go to the publishing house office, and Payot urges me to give him *Le Chamanisme* next spring. Whatever people may say, he's a strange man. After asking me last December to bring him the manuscript of *Prolégomènes* in a few weeks (and I did, having made an effort the effects of which I felt for a long time afterward!), he kept it in his drawer for six months!

26 September

At R.B.'s place to say my good-byes to N.M., who leaves by plane tomorrow for Buenos Aires. Some fifteen or sixteen refugees are there. All they talk about is emigration: to what continent is it possible to go, and how quickly can one obtain an emigration visa? All are in agreement that we *must* leave France, because soon, in a few months or at most a year, Russia will occupy all of Europe.

October

I've taken up *Le Mythe de l'éternel retour* again. I understand with greater clarity than ever the meaning of the last chapter, but I hesitate to open here, in a few pages, the "problem of *History.*" And yet I must. All around me everyone is asking, *how much time* do we have left, when will "they" come?

* * *

I go to Saulchoir to meet Père de Menasce and make the acquaintance of the group Eau Vive. The forest on a cloudy evening. . . . I visit the monastery. There are two hundred monks here, but not a footstep, not a voice can be heard. A silence, total and unreal. P. de Menasce told me that only here, at Saulchoir, does he recover peace of mind and especially the "liturgical spirit," without which his existence would become almost unbearable.

November

For several days it's been so cold in my room at Hôtel de Suède during my working hours that I've been quite uncomfortable. After half and hour, I'm frozen. Now of all times when I'm redacting the conclusion to the last chapter of *Le Mythe de l'éternel retour*!

18 November

Twenty years ago today, at 3:30 (I believe!), I left from North Station in Bucharest on my journey to India. I can see the departure even now: Ionel Jianu with the book by Jacques Rivière and the pack of cigarettes—his last gifts. I had two small suitcases. The influence of that journey, when I was not yet twenty-two. . . . How would my life have developed without my "Indian experience" at the beginning of young adulthood? And the assurance I've cherished ever since, that *whatever* may happen, there is always a cave in Himalaya waiting for me. . . .

18 January 1949

I do "press service" for *Traité d'histoire des religions*, which appears this afternoon in the first bookstores.

24 January

Brice Parain is enthusiastic about *Maitreyi*, which he has read in the German translation. Tomorrow there will be a meeting of the editors at the publishing house, and he assures me that he will insist the novel be engaged and immediately translated.

But still I wonder if it's a good idea to try my "literary luck" in France today with a novel written in 1932, one which does not even represent my Indian experience in its totality, to say nothing of the totality of my literary production. *Maitreyi* has its place alongside my other six or seven novels, but how many of them will have the luck to be translated? Brice Parain urges me to "redeem" my works written in Romanian—but how? Who would translate those thousands of pages? I, at any rate, wouldn't venture to do it. It seems to me more important—and more urgent—to write the books I have "in my head," which I've kept postponing for so many years.

10 February

". . . Voilà que vous nous avez donné enfin un *Traité d'histoire des religions* conçu à un point de vue religieux! . . . C'est un ouvrage de premier ordre, dont on peut dès maintenant envisager l'importance." [Behold, you have given us at last a "treatise on the history of religions" conceived from a religious viewpoint! . . . It is a first-class work whose importance from now on one can envisage], etc., etc., my old master, R. Pettazzoni, writes me.

I remember that morning in 1925 when I discovered *I Misteri,* and I threw myself into the study of the history of religions with the passion and faith of a boy of eighteen. I remember the summer of 1926, after I had begun to correspond with Pettazzoni, when I received *Dio* as a gift from him, and I read it, underscoring almost every line. I remember. . . .

16 February

A meeting today in my hotel room with about fifteen Romanian intellectuals and students. I had called them together to talk about this problem: whether or not we are agreed that *today,* and even more so *tomorrow,* the "intellectual," simply by virtue of the fact that he has access to concepts, is and will be increasingly considered the number-one enemy and that history has entrusted to him (for how many hours?) *a political mission.* In the religious war in which we find ourselves engaged, the adversary is impeded by none but the "elite," who have the advantage, for a well-organized police force, of being rather easily suppressed. Thus, today, the only effective politics available to exiles is to "create culture." Traditional positions are reversed: it is not the "petty politicians" who find themselves at the center of the historically concrete but the learned, the "intellectual elites." (A long discussion, which I must write up one day.)

19 February

At Dr. Hunwald's place I meet Frank Duquesne, the author of the much discussed book, *Cosmos et gloire*. Of Jewish ancestry, through his mother a descendant of H. Heine, yet born a Christian. He was anti-Semitic at fifteen, but he discovered Judaism when he regained his faith. Formerly Greek Orthodox, he now is Catholic, but his passion is esotericism. He gives us to understand that his mission is to revive the esoteric symbolism in Catholicism. His readings are enormous, but they suffer from the shortcomings and omissions of the self-taught. He is too quick to find correspondences, symmetries, and influences. A prodigious memory, imagination, élan. But how many bad books he ingested in his youth and has failed to forget! Fat, with the face of abbot; rather energetic, with brusque, bullish gestures. He took off his jacket because of the heat, rolled up his shirt-sleeves, and smoked a large Belgian pipe. When he isn't speaking, he soon becomes very impatient.

21 February

The sinologist Paul Demieville asked Puech: "Where does Eliade find all his references?" "Indeed," Puech adds, after reporting the question, "what *is* your system for working? How do you document? You give the impression that nothing escapes you, that you've examined everything and read everything. How do you do it?"

I explained that, belonging to a minor culture where dilettantism and improvization are almost fatal, I embarked upon the scientific life full of all sorts of "complexes," constantly fearful that I might not be informed up to the moment. This has prevented me, for as long as I can remember, from sending a manuscript to the printer before I was certain I had read virtually everything written on the problem. I had the horror of not "discovering" things long known, of repeating observations made by others, and, above all, of ignoring some fundamental document buried in a little-known series unobtainable in Romanian libraries. That is why I didn't dare publish a text until I could spend part of a summer in one of the great European libraries.

3 April

This morning, at Gare de Lyon, with *Traité* under my arm for identification, I met R. Pettazzoni (he was carrying *La Religione nella Grecia antica*). At last, after nearly half a century of correspondence, we meet! We talked till 3:00 P.M. when he had to take the train for Brussels. A true "historicist," he resists my attempts to isolate and describe the structures of religious phenomena; but he keeps apologizing all the while, adding that such an effort will renew historico-religious studies.

18 May

I've written nothing in this notebook for several weeks because I have been totally immersed in analyzing, classifying, and completing the materials on shamanism, gathered in the last nine years. Every day, at the Musée de l'Homme. Have opened the notebook in order to record that today I received the corrected proof copy of *Le Mythe de l'éternel retour*.

25 May

Am continuing to work, day and night, on shamanism. Sometimes I feel almost crushed by the massive Soviet ethnographic production. And since I can't see a problem clearly until I see it whole, I keep putting off writing until the last moment, until I've verified even the smallest detail (verifications which often are futile because I can't use them; at most, I content myself with an allusion in a footnote). Another danger: sometimes my "enthusiasm" is exhausted in the research itself, and when I decide to write it up, I compose somewhat reluctantly, hastily, using only a small part of the documentation I've collected and spent days mulling over.

My inclination is to bring out *le côté spirituel,* the symbolism and inner coherence of religious ethnological phenomena, not because I mean to deny or minimize the other aspects—"material," economic, historical, etc.—but because these latter seem obvious to me, whereas the "spiritual side" must be read, so to speak, "between the lines." Besides, a great deal has been written already about the exterior aspects—which often are only parasites on the religious phenomenon.

26 May

Observations by A. Geholen about the hand of the monkey: it is much better adapted to trees than is man's hand, yet it is not "inventive"; it is an arrested perfection, a perfect form which can develop no further. Man's hand, however, is an imperfect, "open" form which is creative precisely because of its failures and semisuccesses.

Analogous to "perfect books": they have said everything, have exhausted the subject by virtue of their having appeared. Imperfect, contradictory works—even confused ones—sometimes open roads to *a different way of knowing,* previously unsuspected.

4 June

Nothing new aside from the exhausting work on shamanism. I've finished the chapter on the symbolism of the shamanic costume. I believe I've succeeded in showing that such a costume constitutes not only a hierophany but also a microcosm. When the shaman dons his costume, he leaves the "profane" world. When he begins to beat the ritual drum, he is already quite far away, "running" or "flying" to the Center of the World. It would please me if this book, *Le Chamanisme et les techniques archaiques de l'extase,* would be read by a few poets, dramatists, literary critics, and painters. Perhaps some of them would profit more from the reading of it than would certain orientalists and historians of religions. . . .

6 June

I awake this morning to the beginning of summer. The sky is crystalline. After so much rain, my eyelids quiver at the light. I gaze hungrily at the park outside my window. How I yearn for "nature," for big trees with gigantic branches! Thoughts of *Le Chamanisme* disturb me. How much longer will I be able to work? I've promised myself to join Christinel at Capri toward the end of the month.

16 June

I receive a postcard today from Benedetto Croce, by which he thanks me for *Le Mythe de l'éternel retour*. He points out that I ought not accord any importance to that little work of Adriano Telgher opposing historicism. He is sending me also a recent article, a "philosophical novel" about the last months of Hegel's life—a novel which, he writes, he amused himself by composing at age eighty-four!

I have received enthusiastic letters from Henri de Lubac and Karl Meuli, and one from Bréhier, full of reservations about "obsolete myths" which are having "so much success" today.

21 June

The summer solstice and the Night of St. John still hold for me all their charms and enchantments. *Something happens*—and this day seems not only longer but purely and simply *different* from the day before or the day after.

Once, in Portugal, I imagined a story about the miracle of regeneration and eternal youth obtained on a Night of St. John. "Imagined" it is an understatement. For many days in a row I seemed to be living under the spell of that mystery. I lived expecting something to happen to me, something to be revealed to me.

* * *

I resumed work on *Le Chamanisme,* working till 4:00 A.M. Finished transcribing the chapter on the symbolism of the shamanic costume. Other chapters sketched and partially written. As usual, I'm paralyzed in that "critical moment" between dusk and dark, from about 8:30 till 9:30. A terrible melancholy, loneliness, and the flavor of futility through my whole being, as though carried in the bloodstream. Only when night has fallen do I return to my senses. Reconciled, I set to work again.

26 June

Sunday. Glorious day!* This afternoon, at l'Abbaye de Royaumont, by invitation of Mme. de F. to hear the last concert in the series
"Semaines musicales internationales." Riding there on the bus through
meadows studded with poppies, I suddenly awake as from a dream,
stirred, because I see before me the landscapes of my childhood; I find
again the sky and fields of Romania. Once more I realize how much my
work and erudition defend me from my longing for the soil and the air
from which I have been separated.

A peaceful, solemn day in the park of that abbey, mute in its ruins.
The concert is held in what formerly was the refectory. But nothing I
heard could banish the thrill I had at first, on my sudden incursion into
the Forest and Summer. Here, my book on shamanism seems to be
ludicrous and—as it really is—a bitter, desperate struggle against time.

Returning from the abbey on the bus, I "see" a novel which
fascinates me to such an extent that I wonder whether I ought not begin
to write it immediately. At first I proposed to take advantage of my
liberation from "science" to see what I could do with my manuscripts
broken off long ago—in particular, *Apocalips*. But the attempt disillu-
sioned me, and I had to invent ad hoc a novel, with the "filming" of
which I entertained myself until we reached Paris.

27 June

All day, somehow in a state of grace. I "see" wonderfully the
beginning and ending of the novel. I know only vaguely what will
happen between that beginning and ending (1936–37 to 1948–49):
twelve years of Romanian life. I'd like to utilize much of what I have
seen and have heard from others, but I especially want to let myself be
carried by imagination and to regain, as in a dream, that paradisiacal
time of the Bucharest of my youth.

I even begin chapter 1. I write three pages. Am dismayed at the fact
that it's going too fast, that my pencil races across the paper. Not

---

*English in the original—Trans.

intending to write more than 600 pages, I must find a slow cadence, a condensed prose. But at 6:30 I meet with Michel Carrouges, and at 8:30 I dine with Turdeanu. I see Herescu at 11:00. It's past midnight when I reach home. Fortunately, my neighbor in room no. 18 has gone to bed. No danger of hearing him making his toilet, coughing, brushing his teeth. I don't feel tired, but I'm too excited to be able to write. I try to finish outlining the next chapters; I note a few particulars. Close to 1:00, I take up *Le Chamanisme*.

If only I could work on both books simultaneously! If I could, for instance, devote afternoons to *Le Chamanisme* and after midnight work on the novel.

28 June

On the way to Musée Guimet I discovered how I could integrate into *Noaptea de Sânziene* (that's what I'm calling my new novel) a good part of *Apocalips,* that is, all the significant episodes. I'm giving up all of part I, Vădastra in lycée and the university. The meeting with Ştefan will occur possibly just because their hotel rooms adjoin (I'll use some of my experiences with the tenant in room no. 18). In this way I'm delivered from a "work in progress" that's obsessed me for many years. And yet I'm salvaging at least 100 to 120 pages out of the 300 or so written.*

I'd have written rather well today (because just as I reached the museum, I realized that on Tuesdays it is closed) had I not had a visit from Lucentini at 6:00, and if M.F., passing through Paris, hadn't caught me on the telephone at 8:00. I go to see him at 10:00 at Hôtel Terminus, near S. Lazare. Paul Mus and Chandra, press attaché to the Indian embassy, were there too. Discussions about scientific trifles and metaphysical abysses. Paul Mus with his timid, tormented smile. Not until after midnight do I return home. I wonder what I'll be able to do now.

3 July

Have stopped work on the shamanism book and am working full time at *Noaptea de Sânziene*. A little while ago I bought this ballpoint

---

Apocalips, begun on 12 December 1942, was definitively abandoned in the spring of 1944 [author's note].

pen because I used up three pencils during the past few days. In this way I'm trying to save my manuscripts from becoming illegible after a few days, as they do now.

Satisfied with that I've accomplished. Over thirty large pages. I've settled on the technique from that chapter in *Huliganii* which Mihail Sebastian liked so much: highly concentrated, almost fragmentary scenes. Only thus will it be possible for me to cover twelve years in seven to eight hundred pages. Danger of letting myself be drawn into fragments of dialogues with "philosophical meaning." Must make an effort to seem mediocre, passing over "weighty subjects" without delving into them. Otherwise, I'll require two thousand pages.

5 July

It suddenly occurs to me that it was exactly twenty years ago, in the heat of Calcutta, that I wrote the chapter, "The Dream of a Summer's Night," for *Isabel și apele diavolului*. The same solstical dream, though with a different structure and played out on different planes, is found also at the center of *Noaptea de Sânziene*. Can this be a mere coincidence? The myth and symbol of the solstice has obsessed me for a great many years. I'd forgotten, however, that it had followed me since *Isabel*.

9 July

The extraction of a molar interrupts work on the novel. I have, besides, a number of little things to finish. I begin the preface requested by Payot for the Laviosa Zambotti book [*Les Origines et la diffusion de la civilisation*]. On the agenda: an article for *Critique* and a review of the monograph, *The Gate of Horn* for *Bibliotheca orientalis*. Then, Capri!

13 July

Tomorrow evening I leave for Capri. For several days I've written nothing more on the novel. I still have to finish reading the translation of *Maitreyi* that A. Guillermou brought me a few days ago.

I take down the fourth volume of Julien Green's *Journal* and turn to the pages for the beginning of 1943, trying as usual to recall events of my life and my reactions from that time. I fall on this sentence: ''Je ne sais pourquoi je note ces petites choses; c'est peut-être l'éternel dèsir d'emprisonner avec des mots l'instant que passe.'' [I don't know why I record these little things; maybe it's the eternal desire to imprison with words the passing moment] (p. 15). I believe that in this thirst to ''save'' the moment lies the whole secret of the fascination of Julien Green's *Journal*. Otherwise, his pages, especially those of the last two volumes, are rather commonplace.

GENOA, *15 July*

Oleanders of my adolescence. Rediscovering Italy, I ask myself how I could have allowed so many years to pass without seeing it again.

PARIS, *12 September*

I returned the day before yesterday. After carrying this notebook around with me for almost two months, I wrote virtually nothing in it.

At Capri I had scarcely any vacation. A few days after arriving, I took up the novel again. In some forty days of work, I arrived at page 302, the bombardment of London. I had already written, I believe, some forty or fifty pages in Paris, and I salvaged a total of eighty pages or so from *Apocalips*.

13 September

I did not go, as I had said I would, to Royaumont. Sick all day. I haven't reaccustomed myself to the menu of the cheap restaurant. I try to make corrections on the novel. It's coming along, but rather slowly. It doesn't seem nearly as good as I'd expected. But I'm afraid that this impression means something else: it could be a sign that I'm becoming detached from literature.

All day, overcast and oppressive. At nightfall, a long, hard rain of late summer, and yet suggestive also of autumn. I stand for a long time at the window. Then I hear my neighbor in room no. 18, and I return to my desk. I have a considerable number of letters to write.

14 September

At Royaumont. I take part in the first discussion. Rain. I shut myself away in my room and make corrections on the novel. Discouraged sometimes by certain ineffectual passages. I shall have to redo it all.

15 September

I slept rather badly, with the moon in my face and annoyed by mosquitoes—but most of all dissatisfied with what I had read in the evening. Following the text closely in order to correct it sentence by sentence, I'm still not sure to what extent my disappointment is due to the unskillfulness of the details or to the mediocrity of the whole. I'm afraid the action in the first hundred pages is too fragmented, almost pulverized as it is into tiny, minute episodes. Then too—and this seems to me very serious—there is a glaring discrepancy between the Vădastra episode (written in 1942) and the rest of the novel. The former is elaborate, "realistic"; the rest condensed, allusive. I must take up the work done at Capri again, reduce Vădastra's "bulkiness," bring him down to size.

The action will be concluded on 21 June 1948, instead of 1949. A perfect cycle of twelve years. In French translation the novel might be entitled, *La Grande année.*

27 September

Bad day. I read Orwell's *1984,* which depressed me to the marrow of my bones. Since yesterday I've been back at correcting the novel. I'd detached myself from it because I had floundered on two or three mediocre and artificially written episodes. I shall have to discard them.

3 October

Have finished the corrections and additions to the novel.

Today Père Bruno from *Etudes carmélitaines* came to invite me to the congress on the theme, "Chasteté et états mystiques" in September 1950.

Eugenio d'Ors sends me yet another article about *Le Mythe de l'éternel retour.* The title: "Se trata de un libro muy importante." More than any other critic whose comments I've had the opportunity to see, d'Ors is enthusiastic because I have brought out the Platonic structure of archaic and traditional ("folk") ontologies. But I am still waiting for the other side of my interpretation to be understood, that concerning the ritual abolition of time and, hence, the necessity of "repetition." The discussions I've seen so far have disappointed me.

5 October

I work on the novel, but rather little. Plagued by essays and studies which must be written by the end of the week. I also have the chapter from *Le Chamanisme* to correct and transcribe for Dumézil.

20 October

I discover that during the night I was robbed. All the clothes I had left from Portugal—six shirts—taken together with the suitcase and the two pens that were on the desk. The thief worked quietly, opened the suitcases, picked out the things that pleased him, left on the bed two summer suits and a dinner jacket that didn't interest him, and went downstairs without disturbing anyone. Unable to estimate the damage—not to mention the annoyance at the police station where the hotel manager sends me to lodge a complaint, etc.

21 October

Still no one has come to investigate the theft, twenty-eight hours after I filed the complaint at the police station. I don't dare leave the building. I wait. For several days just before this mishap I'd been working very well on the novel.

23 October

Cold and rainy for several days. Autumn has passed without my being aware of it. This evening at Henry Corbin's place. He had looked for me several times last week. I saw him the first time on the day of the burglary, but we didn't attempt a serious conversation—we had too many things to say to each other. Today he showed me his copies of *Traité* and *Le Mythe,* read and underscored. He thinks we ought to revive, in collaboration, the journal *Zalmoxis,* with which he is familiar. He reminds me that I published there the long article on alchemy, some years before Jung had discovered the importance of that problem. Mild-mannered, exceptionally learned, and an enthusiast on the subject of angelology. He is returning soon to Teheran where he has lived for several years. Paris seems not to tempt him.

27 October
        In spite of the flu and harassments from all sides, I have continued to write almost every day, laboriously, stubbornly. Today, I've begun making corrections on the typed copy. Rather well satisfied. Will have to rewrite the first ten pages one more time, though.

For the past ten days I've been thinking constantly about "the art of the novel." Whenever I've wanted to continue writing the way I'm writing now, I haven't had the chance. When I "see" a novel in its main lines (more precisely, when I see the beginning and the chief character), I start to write it. And the novel is created as I go along writing it down. That is why, especially in my older novels, there are hesitations, inconsistencies, and much padding. I improvise each evening what I plan to write that night. Sometimes I commence a chapter without knowing what will happen, what characters will intrude, etc.

If I had the patience to write a novel twice, or if I spent more time "filming" it mentally and selecting the most significant and most intense episodes, perhaps I too might become a "true novelist." But, as is the case with my lectures for classes and conferences, I am "inspired" only when I see a thing *for the first time.* All that is pondered, filtered, and revised I find artificial. I must divest myself of this remnant of immaturity, this superstition of "authenticity" at all costs. (Authenticity, I mean, of my aesthetic emotion; I cannot write if beforehand I have made mentally a "general rehearsal" of the scene I have to write. The aesthetic emotion, exhausted by the "general rehearsal," has lost for me its authenticity and spontaneity.)

29 October

Superb day, though cold. A golden light. I go for the second time to the Gauguin exposition. I remember the deep thrill I felt viewing my first Gauguin canvas at the Louvre four years ago.

I read several reviews of *Le Mythe de l'éternel retour*—all excellent. But I have the impression that the most important thesis—the necessity of "repetition," i.e., the periodic recreation of the world—is not understood. The function of repetition (through ritual) is "existential": it is the desire to *continue life*, the hope to prolong it ad infinitum.

31 October

For two days it's been so cold that my hand freezes to the pen. I hold a bottle of hot water on my lap to thaw out my fingers from time to time.

Have worked little and badly on the novel. But I've succeeded in seeing certain scenes clearly. And, even more important, I've seen where danger lies and how I must guard against it. In no event must I ever again write episodes and fragments at random, as "inspiration" leads me. If I were a self-respecting writer, I'd rewrite everything I've written up to this time.

3 November

Stig Wikander has come to Paris. He's staying in my hotel. That means we'll be discussing Indian matters until midnight every night—and the novel will be neglected. I am incapable of *existing* concurrently in two spiritual universes: that of literature and that of science. This is my fundamental weakness: I can't remain "awake" and live at the same time in a state of dreaming, of play. Once I begin to "make literature," I find myself in another universe; I name it oneiric, because it has another temporal structure and because, above all, my relationships with the personages are of an imaginary rather than a critical nature.

13 November

Yesterday and today I wrote those pages which conclude the episode of Ştefan at Lisbon. Am surprised to observe, *après coup,* that

the images that have dominated Ştefan's adventure with Stella Zissu
repeat, in a way, the episode of Ulysses with Calypso.

23 November

For the past week I've been writing rather well, as much as
three or four pages every day. This makes, I believe, over 450 pages
of manuscript. Thus, I've surpassed the thickest of my novels,
Huliganii! I shall have to be more careful, to condense as much as
possible.

29 November

For several days, paralyzed by a new attack of vagatonia.
Drowsiness, abulia. I interrupted work on the novel just when I was
most "inspired."

2 December

Trapped, pressured, overworked—I managed to write only two
or three pages between 2:00 and 4:00 A.M.

Spaltmann writes me his impressions of the first 360 pages of
typescript. He seems satisfied—but not enthusiastic. He remarks, quite
rightly, that Vădastra is the most successful of all the characters. I reply
immediately: the reason is that I took him ready-made from *Apocalips*
and that I have accorded to him alone almost a third of the 360 pages.
Beside him, all the other characters seem improvised.

9 January 1950

Today, our wedding. The witness, N. I. Herescu; the sponsors,
Sibylle and Emil Cioran. Then to 4 rue Mignard. Among the guests: the
Dumézils, the Puechs, and Stig Wikander. The religious service was
celebrated in the parlor (the Romanian church being still closed). I have
rented another room at Hôtel de Suède.

January

Lectures at Collège philosophique (13 and 20 January) on "La
Structure des mythes" and "Le Mythe dans le monde moderne."

I take lunch at Etudes, 15 rue Monsieur, in order to meet Père
Teilhard de Chardin (23 January). Afterward, in his room, a two-hour
discussion; P. P. Fessard, Daniélou, and Bernardt also present. I have
recorded in another place all that Père Teilhard said to me about the
religious ("Christic") value of science and technology, about the
"scientific" arguments that may be adduced to demonstrate the
necessity for the immortality of the soul, and especially about his great
faith in the future and the progress of mankind. Smiling, I tell him that
his Christo-cosmic vision is bolder than the most fantastic Mahayanist
creations (millions of universes, millions of reincarnations, millions of
Bodhisattvas, etc.)—and he agrees; so it is: "science" and the Christian
Logos surpass in their profundity and audacity all that has been thought
or imagined heretofore. . . . As we are parting, he gives me several
mimeographed texts, some in multiple copies, to share with my friends.
The texts, he explains, are some that cannot yet be *published,* but only
duplicated and distributed in select circles.

* * *

I have broken off work on the novel, having written almost nothing
during December and nothing at all during January. Readings: shamanism, Goethe. Many lectures (for Romanians, especially), the only
significant one on Eminescu.

February

Nothing but bad news recently. Since January, General Rǎdescu
has cut off subsidies for intellectuals and students.

* * *

I'm working with enthusiasm—and sometimes with exasperation—
on *Le Chamanisme.* To keep from getting lost in the dozens of files and
the two-thousand-plus pages of notes and extracts, I've decided to
destroy the documentation for each chapter as soon as I've corrected
and transcribed it.

1 March

I was expecting to receive the corrected proof copy of *Maitreyi*
when Brice Parain writes me today that he doesn't like the title, and he
proposes *Amour bengali* or something of the sort. I gather that the book

has not yet been printed and that it won't appear before May. . . . And now I must find a new title!

5 *March*

I interrupt work on the book in order to draft the two lectures I am to give in Rome: "Le Chamanisme" (at the University, on invitation of Pettazzoni) and "Le Tantrisme et le chamanisme" (at Tucci's Oriental Institute).

ROME, *23 March*

ISMEO (Istituto per il medio ed estremo Oriente) had lodged us at Pensione Huber on Via Paisiello, two steps from Villa Borghese. The day after our arrival, a twelve-hour general strike. I can't see Tucci, but I manage to reach Pettazzoni's place, nevertheless. He tells me that he wants to hold the conference in the Aula Prima and that the rector and many other colleagues of his will come. And, indeed, a rather large crowd came. I met or renewed acquaintances with a good number of orientalists, ethnologists, classicists, and historians of religions.

That morning I saw Tucci at the university. He is unchanged. The same exuberant yet lucid energy I knew in Calcutta during 1928–31. (The last time I had seen him was on the ship in November 1931, when we were returning to Europe.) After the lecture he invited us to his house. An immense library and museum. You pass from one room to another—and you think you're in a Tibetan temple! He lives here alone (he is separated from his wife), with a housekeeper and a little dog, which seem to make his loneliness even more obvious. He showed me my books, which he has had bound. It is his proposal that we bring out *Zalmoxis* together, with ISMEO as the publisher. On the invitations to the lecture I gave at the institute, Tucci had written a short and flattering introduction which, in a way, annoyed me, because it "committed" me, it obligated me to devote myself exclusively to orientalistics. I told Christinel: "It's a good thing we're not staying in Rome! I'd find myself back in Indology, I'd be taking up Tibetan again! . . . . But, happily, we saw the forums again, and the ruins, and the villa Borghese.

PARIS, *24 April*

I open this notebook again, having neglected to record so many things (if only it were nothing except the week of vacation we had in Rome, thanks to Tucci, after the lectures), in order to record another mishap: two days ago the cleaning woman somehow—it was my fault—burned three immense file folders containing all the correspondence received in recent months, all the manuscripts of articles for future issues of *Luceăfarul,* and other papers, the exact number and content of which I haven't yet determined. Several kilograms of letters, manuscripts, and notes, which I had set on top of the wastebasket in order to make room on my desk for a cup of tea—and which I forgot about and left there! I especially regret losing the sixty or seventy letters, only a part of which had been answered, from scholars and readers of my books whom I didn't know.

VENICE, *30 May*

Here for three days, having been invited to participate in the Constitutive Assembly of the Société européenne de culture. We are housed in this luxurious hotel, the Bauer-Grünwald (in which almost all of us feel rather awkward). A wave of sadness has come over me suddenly. The last time I was in Venice was in the summer of 1937 when I passed through en route to Berne to see Blaga. All those years spent away from Italy seem sterile and wasted to me now.

I brought this notebook along in the hope that I would open it more often. But only now, three days after arriving, do I succeed in recording a few particulars. I have met, among others, Ungaretti, L. Guilloux, Benda, Mario Praz, Lescure, etc. Long discussions with Abbé Morel, Jean Amrouche, and Jean Wahl.

Evel Gasparini, professor of Slavic studies at the university, who for a number of years has been much interested in ethnology, seeks me out. He tells me that no book has taught him so much as *Traité.* We spend a whole evening in conversation at Riva degli Schiavoni.

1 June

This morning Amrouche tape-recorded a commentary of mine on the initiatory ritual of the labyrinth (apropos of the labyrinth of Stra).

PARIS, *15 July*

For a month and a half I haven't opened this notebook. In all that time, other than intense work on shamanism, a lot of nuissances. *La Nuit bengali (Maitreyi),* already printed several months ago, has been postponed for release until September. But since war broke out in Korea two months ago, God only knows what may happen before fall. I have no money at all; three weeks ago I wrote to M., asking him to grant me a loan for five or six months, but I haven't had a reply as yet. On top of all this, a new attack of "vagotonia" (ever since I was told that, properly speaking, it is not a disease, I always add the quotation marks).

BRIANÇON, *21 July*

Since yesterday, in this vast and curious house at 15 Grande Courbe, in Briançon, Hautes Alpes. An enormous terrace-balcony and before us the valley, houses, and the road.

Fortunately, my "vagotonia" has passed. Among the files lost several months ago was my journal from Cordoba for the autumn of 1944. I wake up in the night sometimes and I remember that incinerated text. It seems to me the best thing I ever wrote. At any rate, it was my most successful "travel diary" of the many I've written and published. At one time, Eugenio d'Ors had the custom of burning each New Year's Eve one unpublished page—*the most beautiful one,* he said. It was his way of *making a sacrifice.* But in the case of my file folders, the "sacrifice" was quite involuntary.*

21 July

The city is squeezed between the walls of the fortress. The main street, las Gargouille, runs down a steep slope; in the middle of it, a

_____
*A few months later I found a copy of the Cordoban journal.

narrow gutter. The children throw wads of paper into it and the water carries them away at an amazing speed.

We walk to the upper side of the city, climbing amid the fortifications. A military hospital and a tuberculosis sanatorium side by side. Several patients "taking the cure" on the terrace are playing cards. A large, ugly statue stands facing a mountain peak. We are told that the statue was given by Americans to the city of Bordeaux but that that municipality refused it for some reason or other. Finally, it ended up in Briançon.

* * *

Since I've recorded almost nothing in this journal for I don't know how long, I haven't recorded the visit I made to Lavastine on one of the last days of June. I met him by chance at Deux-Magots. I was with Christinel and Herescu, taking coffee at 3:00. Lavastine saw me and approached. He was carrying his customary satchel, full of books— some three thousand francs' worth—which he had just purchased. I offered him a cup of coffee. He asked whether he could have coffee with cream and, a minute later, whether he might also have a croissant, because he had had nothing to eat. He had been book buying. . . .

After that I went home with him, and he returned a book he had borrowed from me in 1947. On the way there, he informed me that he was separated from his second wife: she had gone with the children to the United States. His apartment looked much neglected. Several new bookcases had been added. But in his study hundreds of volumes were piled on the floor—books he consulted in preparation for his lectures (he lives on the proceeds from his weekly lectures that bring him four or five thousand francs each).

He asked me to come in a few days to meet a young friend of his who, he said, was under the "evil influence" of a female occultist. It was a very warm night, but I went, and I didn't regret it. A beautiful, dark-complexioned young woman with stunning black eyes. Her "disciple" was also with her: a big oaf of a fellow. The mistress recounted quite calmly, smiling, how during sleep a double of herself is produced and appears to acquaintances at great distances away, without her being aware of it always. She is a *"grande initiée"* and knows all about the "Egyptian mysteries"—without having done any reading, purely by intuition. She remembers many of her previous incarnations. Four thousand years ago she lived in Egypt. Often her double is an Egyptian. Even more interesting: in Africa there exists a secret society whose initiates have seen her surrounded by a sort of aura, looking like Nefertiti, but knowing nevertheless her true (i.e., current) identity. Several of these "initiates," "very cultured and enterprising Negroes," left Africa to seek for her in the world at large. After years of searching, they discovered her here in Paris, in her very elegant apartment, with her forty or so disciples (each paying about ten thousand francs for the initiation course, Lavastine told me). She agreed to become the high priestess of the African Secret Society. She transmits her messages through her "double". . . .

All this in the Paris of A.D. 1950 is not only possible but also very profitable.

26 July

We ascend via the téléphérique to 2,500 meters, and then, at the peak, we come to a little frame church building, Notre-Dame-des-Neiges. Entering, we are struck by the smell of a stable. Probably flocks of goats take shelter here during the winter. The chapel was erected by a woman who, having met with an accident at this spot, promised the Virgin a house if she recovered.

We descend to Briançon through a forest. I am reminded of excursions in the Carpathians in my adolescence and youth. All at once I realize that almost all my friends who climbed the mountains with me during those summers are now deceased, having died on the front, in concentration camps, or in prisons. I am one of the two or three survivors of a group of more than twenty young men (in 1933–34 not one of us was thirty). . . .

28 July

I'd like to be able to write at least one more book besides those already begun (the novel and Le Chamanisme): L'Homme comme symbole [Man as Symbol]. No more than 250 pages—without footnotes, just a simple bibliography at the end. I would show the need of man to live in conformity with symbol, with the archetype. I'd insist on the function that the imagination has of spiritual technique, of fulfillment, equilibrium, and fecundation (well-known examples: those neurotics and psychotics who recover their health insofar as they succeed in regaining, through imagination, *the symbolism of their own body.* And a less familiar example: the desperate case of chronic constipation which L.C. cured by suggesting that the patient imagine a defecation of cosmic proportions). To the extent the man of modern societies rediscovers himself in archaic anthropocosmic symbolism, he acquires a new existential dimension. Thus he regains a major and authentic mode of being which defends him from historicistic nihilism, without removing him from "History." It is even possible that History might reveal its true meaning: as the epiphany of a "glorious" human condition.

30 July

A quarter of an hour on a bench in the park at Champ-de-Mars, listening to the municipal band. It was deplorable, and yet there was a sad, infinite charm about it. I felt as though I had awakened in a bathing-resort city at the turn of the century. I remember experiencing the same emotion during the spring of 1945 while listening to a municipal band in that little Portuguese town where I was living, waiting from one hour to the next for news of Germany's surrender. How many plans for "new life" did we make then, each of us! . . . Only five years have passed since then, and again we await anxiously the latest telegrams—this time from the Korean front.

Marie-Madeleine Davy told me that she formerly was Julien Benda's secretary. She didn't have a great deal of work to do: for a few hours each day she had to read to him—while he lay on a couch with his eyes closed—from his own writings. This was his great passion—to hear himself *pronounced* by someone else. He would listen, fascinated, sometimes nodding his head. Then he would get up—and the secretary was free.

1 August

The anxiety I feel about "events"—that is, about the possibility of a third world war—is continuous and subterranean, fed by the sentiment of guilt that I have made a mockery of my opportunities, of my numerous chances to say *what ought to have been said,* to do *what I was prepared to do*—the painful awareness that I have been unable to fulfill my vocation, although I recognized it early in life.

2 August

Balzac confessed: "Il m'est impossible de travailler quand je dois sortir, et je travaille jamais seulement pour une ou deux heures" [It's impossible for me to work when I have to go out, and I never work for one or two hours only]. It's the same with me, exactly. I have given, I believe, nearly a thousand classroom and public lectures in my life, and each one represents at least one afternoon lost from my work time. Immediately preceding lectures, conferences, seminars, or visits, I can't do anything except read. Occasionally I take notes. How I envied Iorga, who would continue working on his books up to the last minute—and then would go on foot to hold his class at the university or deliver a speech at the Chamber of Deputies or get into a car and go to catch a train for Văleni or Paris, and then start writing again— something else, of course—as soon as the locomotive began to move!

PARIS, 5 August

I returned yesterday evening, alone. Christinel stayed behind at Briançon with the family. The room in which we shall have to live from now on suddenly seems smaller, sadder. In the rooms next door, on the right and the left, which were ours also for some time, strangers are now residing. I hear them talking all the while. I try not to listen.

6 August

I said to Herescu today that, in such moments of international crisis and tension as this, we who are exiles from the East ought to *do something.* For example, inform the French government of our resolve to fight, in case of aggression, on the soil of France; not only for France but for the West. He does not at all agree with my suggestion. If it were possible today to isolate ''France'' from ''the West,'' he would fight for the former, out of sentimental motives and in gratitude (for all that France has done for us in the past). But he has no desire to die for a ''West'' which has betrayed us (not only the Romanians but all the peoples of Eastern Europe) and which is not even disposed to defend itself.

7 August

Today Henri Espieux comes to see me—a young man who wrote me a long time ago, asking for an interview. When he fervently recites certain poems in old Provençal, he feels a euphoria of a mystical nature. Has he not rediscovered, without realizing it, certain mantras? he wrote me.

He is a likable young chap, a Provençal poet. We talk a little about mantra, yoga, etc., and then I ask him about his poetry. He writes only in Provençal; he refuses to compose in French. Cultural autonomy for the south is his hope, and he is fighting for the introduction of Provençal into the schools. He shows and gives me several Provençal publications. It was when he was sixteen that he rediscovered his mother tongue. He learned it from books and dictionaries, because he is a functionary in a Paris bank and is thus far from the ''living sources of the language.'' His ideal: to publish in Provençal.

I venture to differ with him, telling him about the many great poets from our area—Eminescu, Blaga, Petöffi, etc.—who are condemned to remain unknown or, at best, simply *names* in Larousse, just because they wrote in provincial languages lacking wide circulation. He, on the other hand, who has had the good fortune to be able to express himself in a universal language, French, turns his back on it and writes in Provençal. I remind him of Bernard Shaw, Yeats, and James Joyce: would they have become writers of world renown if they had written in Gaelic? These examples don't impress him. Provençal is sufficiently distributed: he points out that at least ten million speak it and that almost ten thousand can read it. Besides, it isn't untranslatable. He wants, like

Mistral, to see bilingual editions of the great Provençal poets and perhaps even of his own poems.

11 August

Have begun writing the two lectures for the Eranos conference at Ascona (actually, only one lecture which will require two hours), but I'm working without enthusiasm, constantly asking myself whether I couldn't utilize such and such a text already written or even published. I meet with this same resistance whenever I'm forced to write about problems already discussed in prior works. (Only Croce has the *genius* to keep saying the same thing without repeating himself, in the sense that he doesn't reproduce *exactly* the texts already written, but he writes them again in a *different way.*)

ASCONA, *20 August*

Lodged in Casa Tamaro, facing Lake Maggiore, the guest of Eranos. I meet and get to know Professor Gershom Scholem of the University of Jerusalem, the renowned authority on the Kabbala. Am very flattered to learn that he has read nearly all my books, including even *Yoga* of 1936. A very pleasant face, with large ears that stand out from his head. He speaks broken English with a delightful accent. He tells me many interesting things, and I shall try to record some of them here and now.

I ask him about Gustav Meyrink. He knew him when he was a young man. Meyrink even took him to see the great hermetist writer R. Eisler. Once Meyrink asked Scholem to explain what he (Meyrink) had meant to say in *Der golem,* because he had written certain pages of the book while inspired by esoteric Jewish sources (bad ones, Scholem added), but without understanding what they meant. So Scholem explained to him: being works invented by second-rate authors, unconnected with the source of the authentic tradition, they *had* no meaning!

One day Meyrink asked him: "Do you know where God dwells?" Scholem didn't know. "At the base of the spinal column!" exclaimed Meyrink. He had read *The Serpent Power* by "Avalon" and had been convinced. God was Kundalini, and Kundalini is found lying coiled at the base of the spine! Scholem doesn't know even now, for a certainty, whether Meyrink always believed in his own esoteric writings—or whether he was just amusing himself, because he was not without a sense of humor.

* * *

This evening I meet Professor Paul Radin. The face of a shopkeeper, with an enormous paunch and a jolly disposition. He laughs all the time. He tells me he has bought a copy of *Le Mythe de l'éternel retour*. His wife says that last year, here at Ascona, she looked from her terrace one night and saw a dragon in the garden. It was quite beautiful and had an "amiable" mien. She did not see it again on subsequent nights. In the daytime she searched thoroughly and found no shadow or object which could have created the illusion of a dragon—especially of an "amiable" dragon, Professor Radin added!

21 August

This morning, at Casa Gabriella, home of the elderly Madame Olga Frobe-Kapteyn. A wonderful villa, right on the shore of the lake. Next to it is Casa Eranos, where the conferences are held. The atmosphere is semimundane, semitheosophical. Kerényi speaks without notes, slowly, with emphasis, theatrically, intelligently. Everyone follows his lecture with a dubious attentiveness. Madame Fröbe detains me then for lunch. Fourteen of us sit around a circular table in the garden. Since the majority are speaking German, I have some difficulty following the conversation. At the close of the meal, a secretary announces that the master (Jung) will arrive during the afternoon. A long conversation with Kerényi, whom I much esteem—although I suspect him of seeking to "publicize" himself.

* * *

Another long stroll with the loquacious Scholem. He tells me about the erotico-nihilistic practices of certain Kabbalistic sects and asks me to clarify several aspects of Tantrism. But he talks mostly about meetings he had with Moses Gaster, concerning whose scientific worth he does not have a very high opinion. One day he and Gaster went to the British Museum, and, as soon as they arrived, the old gentleman clapped his hands and called out: "I am Dr. Gaster, and I'm blind. I want to be taken to the director of the Oriental Department!" Two assistants came immediately, took him by the arms, and escorted him there. But the old man could, at that time, see very well. Moreover, he and Scholem had come by bus and on foot, and he had kept up a running commentary on everything happening around them on the way. His eyes did not become weak until a number of years later.

22 August

Today I see Jung. He is in a chaise longue on the terrace, listening through the open window to Scholem's lecture. For a man of seventy-five, he appears in excellent health. From Mme. Corbin I learn some of the rumors that circulate around the great man. Jung has a prodigious appetite and is a great master in culinary matters. Knowing that Mme. Frobe-Kapteyn does not set a very good table, he secretly bought some dainties and treated himself in his room alone at night. But eventually he was found out, and one of his admirers in Ascona sent him yesterday evening, quite surreptitiously, a fried chicken.

Jung told Corbin that he is grief-stricken over the real existence of "flying saucers." Always he believed in the symbolic significance of the circle and the circular; now that "the circle" seems actually to be "realized," it no longer interests him. It seemed infinitely more *real* to him in dreams and myths.

* * *

Lunch today at a trattoria, the guest of Joachim Wach. He is a very small man, thin, feeble. He tells me that in his seminar in Chicago he has been interpreting *Le Mythe* and *Traité*. He would like to do something toward inviting me to the United States, but he doesn't exactly know what or how. Wach relates depressing things about the theoretical level of American universities. Professors of sociology are just now discovering the works and thought of Max Weber.

23 August

I dine with Jung, seated on his left, and we talk from 12:30 until 3:00. He is a fascinating old gentleman, not at all affected, as happy to listen as he is to talk. What should I set down first from that long conversation? Perhaps his bitter disclosures concerning "official science." He is not taken seriously in university milieux. "Savants are not inquisitive men," he states, quoting Anatole France. Professors are content to reiterate what they were taught in their youth, and especially that which does not disturb the equilibrium of their little universe. Etc., etc. . . . But I sense that at the bottom of his heart Jung suffers a little from this indifference. That is why he is so interested in any "savant," from whatever discipline he may come, who takes him seriously, reads him, comments on him.

25 August

Only last night did I finish writing the lecture (cribbing as much as possible from my books). I delivered it this morning: two hours—and I had a "resounding success." This worries me a little. So many scholarly lecturers present. . . .

I am with Jung for lunch again today. He speaks with me about India. Madame Jung asks me what *"en situation"* means—and we begin an elementary course on Existentialism.

A meeting with Barrett from the Bollingen Foundation. Corbin had spoken to him about my financial plight. He may be able to obtain a grant for me—next year! Of course, next year!

28 August

I've hardly had an hour to myself during the past few days. Endless discussions with the Corbins, the Scholems, the Radins, and the Jungs.

This evening I dine with Massignon. We talk for several hours. Terribly voluble! He is, besides, obsessed with pederasty; again and again he brings the conversation around to "young male prostitutes" and so on. He tells me he is more interested in my *Yoga* than in my other books on the history of religions—because he does not find "man" in them. What made me turn to "primitives" and "archaic" peoples? Is it not, perhaps, humanism? Am I not in fact an "Aryan"? He is a "Semite" (he is even circumcised, he confesses). I explain (too long to summarize here), and I believe I convinced him.

Countless details which I ought to record. For instance: he saw the only files of Huysmans which will never be published: his correspondence with the priest who converted him. The priest was a Satanist. On finding this out later, Huysmans prayed to be allowed to pay for the priest's sins. At that time he had the cancer of the throat from which he died three years later. He offered his tremendous suffering as a recompense for the sins of the priest. The file was taken to the Vatican by Massignon.

AMSTERDAM, *5 September*

Very few memories from these two days in Holland. An adventure the first evening, when, arriving by taxi at the address of my host, I find the house locked and have to seek out a hotel. (I found out the next day that the family had not yet returned from vacation.) I am, moreover, rather poorly accommodated: a governess's room with an army cot and no writing stand—and in the morning they give me, only out of shame, a cup of tea.

Almost nothing to note concerning the Congress for the History of Religions. A steady rain. Only now, as I write these lines while seated on a bench outside the Indisch Institut, facing a canal, is the sky clearing. A strange awakening of light and colors. The city begins to look quite different.

I give an improvised presentation on the subject of "Mythes cosmogoniques et guérisons magiques," with a few interesting observations. Filliozat is fascinated. He urges me to write it up and publish it *as quickly as possible*. (Probably he knows why I should. . . .)

6 September

This evening a reception at the Rijksmuseum. There follows, fortunately, a visitation of the most important halls. Three wonderful Vermeer canvases. I have the good luck to find in the collection on loan from the Berlin Museum two more Vermeers, which I remembered vaguely.

However, I look at too many paintings to be able to appreciate them properly. Ruysdael, A. van Ostade, and Jan Steen (in particular, "The

Sick Man" and "The Dentist-Doctor" fascinate me). Must return here after the congress is over.

8 September

From 9:00 A.M. until 10:00 P.M., on a bus tour of the north. Alkmaar and the cheese market. The church. Again, the sentiment that I'm back in a time which, miraculously, has escaped from history.

Toward Wieringermeer, a part of which was once the Zuyderzee and today is fertile, cultivated land. Traces of the destruction caused by the inundation of 1945 when the Germans dynamited the dikes. The sea—the color of lead and coal. The wonderful church at Edam. I manage to be alone in it for a while.

In the evening we stop to eat at Volendam, a place almost suspiciously picturesque. Someone tells me how painters and tourists have brought about the wearing of this "typically Dutch" costume. We eat at the Hotel Spaander, after a long stroll around the port with Pincherele. Our conversation turns to Buonaiuti. I learn that all his papers were burned in accordance with his will. Gone, then, are those letters of mine from India, and one in particular in which I spoke of the terror I was suffering then—it was the summer of 1929—as I was experiencing, *sensing,* "how time passes." (It's strange that only in that letter to Buonaiuti did I dare speak about that experience, the importance of which I did not understand until much later.)

PARIS, *14 September*

I do press service for *La Nuit bengali.*

2 October

Dr. Roger Godel, the cardiologist from Ismailiya, who wrote me last year a long and interesting letter about my books, today pays me a visit. He brings me a manuscript, *Essai sur l'expérience libératrice.* He tells me he is preoccupied with "l'expérience de l'immortalité" which his cardiac patients undergo on the threshold of death: a feeling of serenity, of being "centered," etc. He has observed a number of homologies between cardiac rhythms and archetypal symbols. One of the ideas he develops in his *Essai:* just as the nucleus plays an essential role in atomic physics, so "the Center" is primary for the metapsychology of the "liberated man." One can understand the mode of existence of a *jívan-mukta,* a man "liberated in life," only by taking account of the symbolism of the Center.

11 October

Henry Corbin, whom I have seen several times recently, tells me a terrifying dream. He finds out I've had an accident and am dead. He is disconsolate. A very great sadness. (We had met the night before he had this dream, and I had spoken to him about l'experiénce de l'immortalité.) Then someone comes and tells him he's not sure that I'm dead, that there is still a small hope. He waits, greatly excited. At last the news comes that I'm all right. Some time later in the same dream he finds me. I am stretched out on a couch—dead! This time there's no doubt of it. A crowd of people are around me. Someone comes up and rattles some pieces of metal beside my ear. I revive. . . .

12 October

Dr. René Laforgue, with whom I have had long talks at the Fontainebleau, is going to Casablanca for three months and has lent us his apartment at $62\frac{1}{2}$ rue de la Tour. He invited us to lunch today and showed us the place. I can't believe it! To be able to work without neighbors! We can move in in a day or two. I haven't decided yet whether to give up the lease on room no. 17 in Hôtel de Suède.

27 October

For two weeks, on rue de la Tour. I came here in high spirits, certain I'd be able to resume work on *Le Chamanisme.* But I've been working constantly on other things: the article for *Etudes carmélitainés* (my presentation at the Fontainebleau), the article for *Critique,* and other little things. For several days the sky has been bright, and the air has turned very cold. I warm my hands by blowing on my fists.

I haven't given up the room in Hôtel de Suède. From time to time I go there—to get some correspondence or a few books. The chrysanthemums haven't shed their petals yet; I find them each time just as I left them in the vase by the mirror. But the room seems so bare, so poor—the room in which I felt so comfortable for almost four years.

28 October

On a shelf in the doctor's bookcase I discover a French translation of *War and Peace*. I thumb through it melancholically, struggling all the while with the temptation to reread it. It was exactly ten years ago in Oxford that I read the novel last. Soon afterward I started writing *Viaţă nouă*. How many vain dreams, how many plans, and above all how much work!—all drowned in the same shipwreck that threatens every major enterprise I undertake. During the past ten years I have returned three times to novel writing—only to abandon it after a few months. *Viaţă nouă,* 1940–41; *Apocalips,* 1942–44; and now *Noaptea de Sânziene.* Have I become "short of breath?" Has my "epic vein" gone dry? I can't really believe that. But I have my unfortunate scientific books to finish. And even for them I find less and less time available. Since moving to rue de la Tour I've been working constantly, as much as twelve or fourteen hours a day—all for studies, articles, lectures. I've scarcely done anything on *Le Chamanisme.* I can't imagine when I'll be free again for novel writing.

How many possibilities—squandered on works of minimal importance! How foolishly I've behaved in these recent years of freedom which, by some miracle, have been granted me. Instead of concentrating on my major books and above all on the novel, I expend myself writing lectures, studies, and articles. How I'll regret it later!

17 November

Yesterday evening I received from René Dussaud a letter with a check for two thousand francs! An advance on the second volume of *Traité,* he says. It is a graceful way of helping me. I had written asking him to support my request at Recherche Scientifique—and I told him the truth (but without mentioning the debts I have). Now the problem arises, how do I return the check without offending him? If I'm accepted at Recherche Scientifique, maybe I'll find a means. . . . I've been terribly sad: depressed and humiliated.

25 November

I began working on *Le Chamanisme* on Monday, 20 November. Since then the work has gone rather well. But I've written and transcribed scarcely twenty pages, working between twelve and fourteen hours per day. I remember what Ioan Coman told me in 1938: Iorga, when he was working on *Istoria Românilor* in ten volumes, confided in him once: "I'm writing very slowly, domnule Coman. Hardly fifteen pages a day." Fifteen pages of printing in octavo! And in addition he was writing I don't know how many other books and articles, holding lectures at the university, and giving countless speeches.

1 December

For the past several days the Chinese offensive in Korea has revived the panic that a war is imminent. Suddenly I realize that I have wasted five more months on trifles instead of having the courage to refuse everything else and finish *Le Chamanisme*.

9 December

Yesterday I spent the last of our money (borrowed from so many places!). That evening Christinel went looking for more, and she borrowed another five hundred francs from L. Z. I thought, I can breathe easily for at least a few more days.

But this morning I receive a letter informing me that I have been granted by the Bollingen Foundation a stipend of two hundred dollars per month, beginning the first of January 1951, for three years! I can scarcely believe it! All that's left now is for war to break out—because that's what happened in 1940: I was in London, I had money, but there was nothing I could do with it.

21 December

I haven't opened this notebook for some time. A good sign! I've been working all the while, and better and better. In one month I have written, corrected, and transcribed two chapters totaling almost one hundred large pages. Afternoons I spend at Musée de l'Homme completing my information and checking the documentation gathered years ago.

31 December

The last day of the year, and I find myself working on *Le Chamanisme*. During the past week, despite the holidays and the fact that I was rather tired (because, although I'm free from pain, I'm not entirely over the sickness), I worked steadily and made rather good headway. By stubborn persistence, I maintained an average of three pages per day.

I have tried to calculate in my mind, quickly, the balance for the year 1950. Long periods of "vagotonia" (dizziness, drowsiness, diminished vitality, etc.) in which I was unable to work. Then, numerous articles, book reviews, and lectures which consumed an enormous amount of time. Finally, the four trips. And, in spite of all these things, now, as I make the reckoning, I see that I've written a full three hundred pages of *Le Chamanisme*. Still, if I'd known how to organize the work better, I'd have finished the book last winter and it would be in print now. I'd have been free to concentrate on the novel.

25 March 1951

Easter. I hope we can leave this evening for Italy. Christinel has gone to the station to reserve seats. The rail strike came to an end only last night. The day before yesterday I finished the "Conclusions" to *Le Chamanisme*. The rest of the book was done a week ago. I took it to Payot on March 20. Seven hundred pages in typescript. . . . What a good book it *might* have been if, before I began the "Conclusions," I hadn't been so fatigued and disgusted. Those last fifteen pages I wrote with an immense effort. They turned out vague, mediocre. And, unfortunately, they bear the title "Conclusions." Many people will content themselves with reading only these pages—and they'll ignore the rest of the book, where they would find some admirable chapters.

The fate of all my books: to be concluded in great haste. But I couldn't wait any longer. I wanted to be set free. I haven't any plans for the future. I know only that we're leaving for Italy and Sicily.

The only important event of the winter: the death of Gide.

* * *

A surprising spectacle for an Easter: the bright morning turned gradually to darkness, and now snow is falling. It's falling heavily, thickly, as I haven't seen it snow in a long time.

ROME, *28 March*

I bought this pocket notebook in a tobacco shop next door to the Hoepli Bookstore. Am resolved to record here primarily things that pass through my mind. The "fall-out" of a time which, in the past few days, has changed its rhythm. (Why do I keep putting off "spelling out" that idea which so long has obsessed me: the *transformation* of time experienced through the *changing of the familiar landscape*?)

* * *

I see Pettazzoni today, and again the passion for the history of religions, the interest in erudition return. When I think about the efforts I made two or three weeks ago to finish *Le Chamanisme* and of the "Conclusions" improvised in one evening. . . ! Pettazzoni still hasn't finished his book on the omniscience of God, begun in 1938.

NAPLES, *29 March*

At the Pensione Marguerita, on via Cimarose: we have a room on the top floor with a window overlooking the bay. Tonight Giacomo takes us by car to Pozzuoli and the lakes in the volcano craters. The sinister, leaden light of the cold waters: one ought to travel this region with Virgil in hand! Barbed wire and signs warn that the ground is mined: all that still remains here of the last war. Naples swallows "historic events" one after another and digests them in her mythic, multidimensional body.

31 March

A half hour short of Villa San Giovanni, the train has been standing for a long time in a station the name of which I can't see. The passengers are beginning to get out. I have just learned the reason for the delay: someone committed suicide a few minutes before by throwing himself under the locomotive.

Not far away the sea can be seen between the orange trees. Now, as dusk comes on, the sky is clearing. We have been passing through orange groves laden with fruit.

TAORMINA

We ascend the hill to Hotel Miramare by car. Dark, cold. But the fragrance of the many flowers fairly stupefies us. We try to distinguish among them: orange blossoms, Queen of the Night, wallflowers. Inside the hotel it is warm. The atmosphere of evening. A magnificent terrace.

TAORMINA, *1 April*

The piazza, with three orange trees by the entrance. Two other piazzas, the last one with a fountain and sea horses. In the window of a nearby photographer, a picture of the fountain and a young man with an arm thrown around one of the sea horses, bears this caption: "X. Y., il famoso scrittore inglese." I don't recall the name of this "famous author": in fact, I've never heard of him.

* * *

Ruins. All this part of the city suffered bombardment. Two churches and countless houses standing with the windows blown out. Right on the brow of the cliff, a house broken in half: one half collapsed, the other stubbornly standing, seemingly waiting to fall. But weeds have begun to grow on the roof, the balcony, and the window ledges, and in ten or fifteen years it could become almost a "romantic ruins," even beautiful. But Taormina is rapidly being rebuilt.

Etna, lifting its peak into the clouds. . . .

2 April

The first sunny day. We climb to the Madonna del Monte, stopping frequently to look down on the city, its buildings clustered as in a mountain hollow. Clearly visible are the ruins of the ancient theater. Yesterday afternoon we spent a long time there. There were several Anglo-Saxon couples roaming around it in a state of bliss. A young man, seated on a rock, was sketching the columns. Below, by the gate, a woman of indefinite age was writing letters.

* * *

We climb and then we look from a parapet at the other side of Taormina, facing Etna. We descend by the roadway. An unfinished house already has flowers in the planters and a wisteria vine in bloom. I said to myself that I could come here to write. I've already written thirty-five picture postcards and two letters. Today I get my revenge as best I can: I keep opening this notebook.

I regret my inability to transmit into memory, by means of these notes, a plenitude, a total vision: for instance, the sea viewed from the terrace or, from up on the mountain, the panorama of the two or three successive bays. I'm incapable of "expressing" such global images or—I might dare say—such hours, such units of concrete time. I can record in this notebook only events and, lacking these, fragments of a vision.

* * *

Sometime I'd like to try that experiment of Eugenio d'Ors, described in his *Oceanography of Boredom:* in the sunshine, with eyes closed, to comprehend, to express, to synthesize. What? That total experience of a flux which comes from all directions and then disappears, without our knowing how, into nothingness, nonbeing.

* * *

I often return in thought to my novel. A great many passages seem strident. I keep asking myself, how can anyone write naturally, simply, "credibly" about things so "great" as the passage of time, love, and the miracle of events?—and do it without resorting to the two thousand pages to which Tolstoi was entitled?

3 April

To Catania and Syracuse on the CIT bus. Black rock cliffs: the Cyclopes. Arcireale. The castle on the seashore: black, medieval. An alien presence in this Mediterranean landscape.

* * *

We are passing now through Catania, where we shall stop on our return this evening. Ten minutes in the piazza near the Dome. The Germans in the seat ahead of us keep eating their sandwiches. Two elderly American ladies, dressed manishly, have alighted from the bus in order to read their Baedeker in the sunlight on the sidewalk. A flock of pigeons suddenly takes flight. Trams stop beside us: I'd like to fix in my mind one of these faces that follow us with their eyes; I'd like to remember it later. The man with the short beard, black hat, and a *cestino* in his hand. He gets off the tram and boards our bus. It was he for whom we were waiting. Now we leave for Syracuse.

* * *

We separate from the sea, turning our backs on it. Along the road and on the heights the concrete domes multiply. Here the German sentinels watched in anticipation of an invasion.

Orange groves. Steep cliffs. The road ascends vertiginously, in a spiral. On the flank of a valley, the large country villa of a wealthy landowner; below it lie groves of lemons and oranges. Alongside, an old wall, half-burnt and overgrown with weeds.

. . . Why am I recording all these trifles?

* * *

Fifteen kilometers from Syracuse the landscape changes again. We have descended from the rocky heights. Gardens and woods become numerous. We pass down a long, amazing, shady lane. A great many flowers. We go directly to the Greek theater. To the right, far away, rise the mountains; behind, the sea. For the first time, the Sicilian sun seems blinding. I imagine many things. . . . I dream. Useless to write.

Here and there, a red poppy among the rocks. Lizards. Half-obliterated Greek inscriptions. I can't bear to leave this amphitheater so well-preserved. Dionysos's Ear: the echo. A group of English people with the CIT guide, who pronounces words slowly so they can hear the echo. This cave, these gigantic crevices, and the thick, wild vegetation growing in the shade and dampness—remind me of India.

Syracuse: at the port. The sea seems to me unnaturally calm here in the bay. The houses with their inevitable colored linens hanging at the windows. The sunshine. Naked children ready to go swimming.

Fonte Arethusa, Largo Arethusa. The little basin full of fish.

The two elderly Englishwomen who refused to pay the forty-lira admission fee to the cavern, Dionysos's Ear, get off at Hotel Politis.

1 9 5 1 *(125)*

* * *

The Temple of Athena, built in the third century B.C. and transformed into a church in the seventh century A.D. One sees from the outside the columns that have been integrated into the walls of the basilica. I don't understand why I'm so moved.

PALERMO, *5 April*

Last night, after our arrival at Hotel Villa Lincoln, a terrible electrical storm kept me awake until almost 2:00.

* * *

With a cabdriver, we tour the city leisurely. Before hiring him, we strolled around the harbor district which was bombed during the war and half razed to the ground. We came out onto a highway along which trees have just been planted. An enormous promenade by the seashore—"all the way to Messina," someone boasted.

* * *

In a park of palms, beneath a cool, deep sky of blue. Suddenly I think of Bălcescu. When he was dying here in Palermo, how did this park look?*

The old gardener: with a white mustache, cane, and a military cap, only very discreetly galooned, with white flowers from the shrubs stuck in it. Nothing but old men on all the benches. They all know one another, undoubtedly. They follow the movements of the gardener with a strange, detached attention.

* * *

In the public garden Flora (or Villa Giulia, as it is also called) Goethe "contemplated" not only the lemon and orange trees but all those species of palms and cacti which allowed him to "see" what he named the *Urpflanze*. (What I wouldn't give to be able to reread *here* that brilliant booklet, *Versuch, die Metamorphose der Pflanzen zur erklären*, from 1790!) Seldom in the history of science has there been more difficulty in recognizing the need for a *method*—perhaps because Goethe himself considered the "original plant" a *scientific* discovery.

*Nicolae Bălcescu (1819–52), Romanian historian, died in Palermo—TRANS.

But when the history of the idea of *morphology* as Goethe understood
it shall be written, it will be seen how fecund it has been, not only in the
natural sciences but also in the classification, analysis, and interpretation of spiritual creations: for example, the graphic arts, folkloric
products, aesthetic concepts, etc. I remember that the Russian folklorist
Vladimir J. Propp cites long passages from Goethe's *Morphologie* as
mottoes for the different chapters in his *Morfologija Skazki* (Leningrad:
1928). But the book has passed unnoticed,* as has also happened with
Lucian Blaga's study of 1925, *Fenomenul originar.* Was it only the fault
of the *material* inaccessibility of these books (*Morfologija Skazki*
published in the "Academia" series and Blaga's work in a language of
minimal currency), or was it the *zeitgeist* of the era between the wars
which opposed this method of delineating structures by reducing
phenomena to "archetypes"?

6 April

I like this large, cool room in Hotel Villa Lincoln. It all reminds
me of Mrs. Perris's rooms on Rippon Street. Houses built for defense
against the heat. Suddenly I'm projected back in time: Calcutta, 1929.
And then, all at once, I sense again in the roof of my mouth, burning
and very bitter, the taste of ashes of *Noaptea de Sâziene.*

* * *

I believe Palermo is one of the few Italian cities that I know well.
Every since we arrived, we've done nothing but walk. The weather
continues to be superb.

The Piazza San Martorano, opposite the university, I particularly
like. Here we waited yesterday for the sunset. This morning I returned
alone after having been to the barber. He had cut my hair so short that
when I looked in the mirror I began to laugh. I didn't recognize myself.
Something similar happened to me once in Calcutta, in the winter of
1929. I didn't speak Bengali and could barely make myself understood
in Urdu. I don't know what the barber thought I had said, but he

*It was discovered after being translated into English in 1950. However, the translator
omitted all the Goethe quotations which had been used as chapter headings—to the great
indignation of Propp [author's note, 1971].

resolutely put the close-cutting clipper at the nape of my neck and in a single movement, before I could protest, ran it up to the top of my head.

* * *

We leave for the harbor in a carriage. Marvelous sunset. The very fact of riding in a carriage projects me back into the fabulous time of my childhood. The trotting of the horses, the night, the pavement of a city street bring back my earliest recollections: when I was three or four, living in Râmnicul Sărat, I sometimes would hear that clop-clopping at a distance. And from my first journey to Bucharest at the same age nothing remains in my memory but the trotting of the carriage horses as they departed slowly into the night.

* * *

The ship did not leave at 6:00, the time printed on the ticket. There is a *sciopero,* a strike, but only of the seamen and firemen of the steamship company. Several officials arrive by automobile, and negotiations begin.

We watch the groups on the dock. I can't take my eyes off a certain elderly woman in particular: how coquettish she is! (With her hair bleached, wearing a large straw hat decorated with flowers and an ''elegant'' fur wrap, in fashion circa 1925. . . .) While clinging to her husband's arm, she is continually casting glances over the heads of the people around her toward the passengers lined up on the deck of the ship. Such admiring looks seem not addressed to travelers to Naples but to voyagers on an ocean liner, about to cross the seven seas—to India, for instance, or Australia, or at least to America. Perhaps the old lady was once a showgirl, or maybe a diva in a provincial cabaret. The mask she persists in preserving is somewhat reminiscent of the make-up of a third-rate singer from around 1920–25.

* * *

The ship leaves an hour late, but immediately the bell rings for dinner.

We gaze at the lights of Palermo. Very soon the ship begins to rock. We go below to the dining room, but Christinel lacks the courage to eat dinner, contenting herself with a sandwich. I, in contrast, have the appetite of a wolf. (I remember how, in December 1931, returning from India via the Adriatic, I was almost alone at the table.)

NAPLES, *8 April*

It is rather dark, but we leave by car with Giacomo. Vesuvius. We cross over mountains—almost touching the clouds—and descend to the sea. We enter Ravello. Then we climb again, and at each hairpin turn of the road we become more fascinated by the little town below, with its white houses. We visit Villa Ruffoli. Am moved from the start by this Germanic tower, somber and "Gothic." It seems to transport me from the Mediterranean to the north, to a region under other skies. Stylistically an Arabic-Germanic mixture. The old vineyard. Palms alongside flat-topped, spreading umbrella pines. Klingsor Garden. The sea glittering below, far away. The tower and the worn-out stairs: *Vietato salire* [ascent forbidden]. Fountains, flowers. . . . I have a crazy urge to refreshen myself on the period of Wagner's life connected with this landscape. Amalfi. The dome. The *chiostro* [cloister]: Arabic style, as at Cordoba. The palms blend into the spaces between the white columns. We go too fast for me to be able to savor all these unique hours. We pass too quickly from one plane to another: the landscape, humanity, history are changed every few minutes.

* * *

Toward Positano. A road of incomparable beauty cut into the mountain over a hundred meters above the sea. Giacomo drives like mad. Sometimes he frightens me. If another car should appear from behind a corner of the rock, we'd all go over the cliff. . . .

We go down into the town of Positano, walking on narrow streets lined with wisteria. The sun is shining, but the sky is half covered with thick clouds. We enter a courtyard of Spanish style. Traces of Iberian influences throughout the region. The church is right on the beach. And beside it a "chic" café-restaurant. A place frequented by "artists."

(Here I break off the transcription of the contents of the pocket notebook. We stayed in Naples three more days, then spent a week in Rome before returning to Paris. We arrived home 20 April.)

PARIS, *24 April*

Today I try to classify my notes and review the texts I'll use for the book on tantrism. My capacity to forget alarms me. "Ideas" and observations set down two or three years ago seem now to have come from someone else; it's as though I had never thought them!

* * *

I find this wonderful phrase in a letter of Balzac: "toute personalité est odieuse quand elle n'est pas accompagnée du pouvoir" [all personality is odious when not accompanied by power].

25 April
Someday I ought to write a "rational history" of my entire scientific-philosophical production, showing the hidden relation that exists among all these works, apparently disparate, and explaining why I wrote them and to what extent they contribute *not* to a "system" but to the foundation of a method.

23 May
Two weeks spent with making corrections and the index for *Le Chamanisme*. Almost nothing of interest. Since we returned from Italy, it has been cold, dark, and rainy nearly every day. "Les saints de glace," they say.

A lecture at l'Institut universitaire roumain, with which I was satisfied: the significance of orientalism for Romanian culture. I must find time someday to write a longer study. Meanwhile, I have to hand over to R. Queneau by the first of July the chapter on "Oral Literature" for the *Histoire de la littérature universele,* vol. 1 (Bibliothèque de la Pléiade), the chapter I promised him four years ago.

1 June
We returned this evening, but for only a month, to $62\frac{1}{2}$ rue de la Tour. I met Dr. René Laforgue about ten days ago; he proposed we return, and I accepted. Since coming back from Italy we have had only room no. 17 at Hôtel de Suède. One of our neighbors wakes me up at 2:00, the other wakes me at 7:00.

9 June
Having finished both the text for Queneau (he had demanded it by June 1, via an ultimatum) and the second proofs of *Le Chamanisme,*

I am "free"! I can hardly believe it. Five glorious days of the beginning of a victorious summer. I went to Versailles. The existence which acquires its savor in retrospect.

Still I hesitate: shall I take up the novel again, prepare the lectures for Ascona, or work on the little volume *Le Tantrisme* promised to Georges Bataille three or four years ago? I tried to reread the beginning of the novel. Impossible! Amazingly artificial. I wonder how I could have *believed* in such pages! I shall have to redo the whole beginning. But how, and when? Not one of the main characters has substance. I wrote while "inspired"—and everything seemed "beautiful" to me because I was dreaming my dream and I didn't see the text I was writing. And, unfortunately, I can't write literature unless I am "inspired." Once I was able to do it, when I was young and obliged to publish in order to live; then I could force myself to finish something I had begun in a moment of euphoria, even after the original inspiration had passed.

* * *

A. Busuioceanu sends me still another article by Eugenio d'Ors: "Del Mito" (*Arriba*, 3 June 1951), in which he speaks enthusiastically about *Le Mythe de l'éternel retour*. But he seems to accuse me of not going deeply enough into the philosophical meaning of my discoveries and of giving too much importance to "erudition." Busuioceanu writes me: "He adds a nuance of impatience to his admiration for your thought. I repeat the words he spoke to me one day recently: 'I wonder whether Mircea Eliade realizes where his discoveries about archetypes can lead?' He is waiting for a sequel to your book. And I have the impression that now, in the twilight of his life, he is experiencing a strange feeling of regret that he didn't write the book you have written. . . ."

12 June

Today I meet Günther Spaltmann, my [German] translator. A man of about thirty-five, blond, broad-shouldered, jovial, given to making sudden rejoinders, widely read, humorous. After our having corresponded for five years and after his having read almost all my books (and having translated six!), we have much to say to each other.

But I challenge him at the outset by bringing up the novel. His reservations about the beginning of it are exactly my own. He suggests a way out: to open the novel with Vădastra. But the key to the whole book lies in the meeting in a forest on the Night of St. John.

He tells me that I ought to devote myself from now on to literature. I have lingered too long in science. After reading my palm, he adds that I ought to hurry. If I do not succeed this year in catching the threads which proceed from my "subconscious," I risk losing the gift of imagination forever. But I will remain lucid, critical, and philosophical till the end of my life.

19 June

I was in torment this whole week, trying to "save" the novel. Sometimes I despaired: it all seemed so irremediably mediocre, artificial, even in bad taste. But I believe I have found, or am on the way to finding, a solution: to abandon the unbelievable events and fairy-tale atmosphere of the first several dozen pages and to present them as only a wish—absurd and yet logical—of Ştefan, and to make the whole action more concentrated. The 500 pages now written must be reduced to 250 or 300. Also, as I had begun to do anyway, I must "flesh out" the principal characters, saturating them in the concrete; they're too hazy and cerebral in the first draft.

I believe, however, that I've learned a lesson: it is possible to write an epic *well* only by writing slowly, continually reviewing the pages written, redoing an episode several times over. Brice Parain was right when, speaking of books (any book) he said to me, after you've finished it, put it in a drawer and start writing it all over again.

24 June

I've succeeded, after two or three attempts, in writing the beginning of the novel. But now it will be necessary to rewrite more than half the manuscript—that is, all that does not pertain to Vădastra.

It's strange, but once I begin to work on this novel, I am gradually engulfed by a mysterious sadness which, eventually, drains me.

29 June

Tomorrow we shall return to Hôtel de Suède. But for only four or five days, because on 5 July we leave for Guétary. We are moving permanently. The rent on the room has been raised again. My heart aches when I think of leaving rue Vaneau. I've lived here four and a half years, and I wrote my first books in French and saw them published while staying here. A whole library to transport, plus suitcases, papers, correspondence.

I've written about forty pages. There have remained in this new redaction only the pages about Vădastra and doamna Porumbache. I still foresee a number of difficulties. Above all, how to make the transition from the direct presentation, in the present tense, of the first version to the concentrated time, the "flashbacks," which I *must* use in order to save the novel.

GUÉTARY, 18 July

Here since 5 July, at Villa Bidé Héguia. On the national highway. For the first few days, incapable of doing any work on account of the noise, but am getting used to it now.

I have reopened this notebook in order to record a short "bulletin" concerning the novel. Am up to page 90. I have incorporated some thirty pages about Vădastra; the rest written almost entirely de novo. But still I haven't succeeded in producing the "beginning of a novel" which I desire: out of the ordinary, moving, and yet plausible. (This whole novel is stigmatized by the false fairytale air I gave it in the first version. Exasperated by the price I must pay for that unfortunate euphoria of two years ago, when I wrote while "inspired.") I had settled on a version which, a week ago, seemed good to me. Rereading it in Christinel's typescript, it depresses me. A few pages excellent; the rest very ordinary, makeshift. It's precisely what aggravated me so much in the 1949 version: it is written just to be written—nothing more. No creative effort. I'm exasperated by the facility I had then, from which I still haven't recovered. I do nothing to discover, to invent. I accept the first solution I see, whatever it may be.

31 July

Tomorrow we return to Paris. My vacation is at an end. In these twenty-five days I've worked constantly, some seven or eight hours each day. Rare excursions to Biarritz, Saint-Jean-de-Luz, and Hendaye. Have reached page 182, and until yesterday or the day before I was satisfied with it. But today I read over a part of the manuscript, and I'm discouraged all over again. Undoubtedly, the new version is clearly superior. Certain passages ''seen'' and written now, seem excellent. I've resolved a good number of difficulties, but I'm struggling with others which paralyze me. First of all, the physical resemblance between Ştefan and Partinie, which is a facile dodge and today exasperates me. (Who made me do it, *who*?!) It's too late now to abandon it. The novel—this whole section of it—is held together by that fatal ''confusion'' due to which Partenie loses his life. Another difficulty: Ştefan's inclination toward ''the fantastic.'' It manifests itself only in certain circumstances; the rest of the time Ştefan is ''normal.'' Hence the incongruities and lack of unity in the novel. Finally, I'm paralyzed by the chronological length of the novel: twelve years. Even with the abuse I make of the technique of concentrated time, I can't avoid those twelve years which are, moreover, years heavily laden with history, the years of the war and the Russian occupation.

I'm furious that I undertook this absurd novel in 1949! I could have resumed writing the sequel to *Huliganii* (with nearly five hundred pages already written!), or I could have invented something else that would have allowed me to express my possibilities. But instead I chose a subject that exasperates me by its difficulties and impossibilities.

Tomorrow I return to Paris and start work on my lectures for Ascona.

PARIS, *5 August*

I'm beginning to understand the source of the sentiment of futility and, sometimes, of panic and despair that comes over me whenever I try to represent the novel to myself as a whole: I see it not only as a novel but also as a historical fresco, a sort of *War and Peace*. Now, herein lies my difficulty. This novel, spread out over twelve years, is also a fresco in a sense, but its center of gravity is situated elsewhere: in the different conceptions of time assumed by the principal characters. If I try to compose a historical fresco, I fail from beginning to end. Not with heroes such as Vădastra or Ştefan can I present a *War and Peace* of contemporary Romania. Such a novel—a historical fresco—I could write, but at another time. In no case could it be *Noaptea de Sânziene*. I must, therefore, have the courage to condense, to "skim over" historical events. Only the destiny of the characters matters—not contemporary history. I believe the reader will notice the passage from the "fantastic time" of the beginning (the meeting in the forest), to the "psychological time" of the first chapters, and, more and more high handedly, to the "historical time" of the end. The ending—the Night of St. John of 1948—brings Ştefan back into the fantastic time of childhood, glimpsed as through a fog in the forest at Băneasa.

8 August

(Note written at Café Viel, waiting for N.I.H.) Why do I relive "that time" whenever I come here? When I sit at a table in any corner of this café, I find again the years 1945–46 when I used to meet here with Lică Gracanera. I find again the "vision of Paris" I had at that time—the excitements, the anticipations, the hopes of my first Parisian months. In particular, I regain the taste of "adventure," the feeling of utter freedom which I lost soon after that (when I began to have a work schedule, engagements, etc.). Here, at the Viel, I find myself again as I was five or six years ago. And I am stirred by the feeling of bliss I had then, that of a man *without a schedule*. (Of course, the bliss is due *also* to the recovery of that fragment of the past.) On the other hand, nothing can equal the plenitude of potentialities, all that lies *ahead, in front* of us. Here, at the Viel, I feel that those five years I had before me then when I was waiting for Lică could have been infinitely fuller, more productive, more happy.

20 August

We are leaving this evening for Ascona. The balance sheet for these twenty days in Paris: I drafted the lecture, "Le Temps et l'éternité dans la pensée indienne"; perhaps more important, I decided to collect in a volume several studies on religious symbolism written in recent years and published in specialist journals. I say "perhaps more important" because I've begun to realize that the opinion of "specialists" does not have the weight I accorded it. A culture is neither enriched nor made poorer if specialists in Indic or Altaic studies accept or reject a certain method. What matters in the historical moment of today is that, on the one hand, we do not fall again into the cultural provincialism and ethnocentrism of the period between the two world wars and that, on the other hand, we *force* the dialogue between disciplines. I am much more interested in the reaction of a philosopher, a literary critic, or a psychologist to his reading of "Le Symbolisme des noeuds" or "Le Temps et éternité dans la pensée indienne" than the comments of my colleagues in Indology and the history of religions. But in this case it is necessary that such texts not remain buried in specialist journals (as happened with my studies published in *Zalmoxis* 1–3 which appeared in 1939–41, the last two volumes of which had a circulation, outside Romania, of twenty or thirty copies; the rest of the edition disappeared in the bombardment of Bucharest in 1944). I must, as soon as possible, correct them, complete them, and gather them in volumes accessible to nonspecialists. I see already a first volume: *Images et symboles,* which I shall propose to Gallimard.

ASCONA, *27 August*

I gave my lecture today, with every great success—although I was afraid that it might be a disaster. Last night I was unable to close my eyes except, intermittently, between 2:00 and 4:00 A.M. After that, impossible to fall asleep. The worst insomnia I can remember. All the more strange since I haven't suffered from insomnia for a good many years. It's curious: I wasn't at all tired—either before, during, or after the lecture. Now, at 11:00 P.M., that same lucid euphoria which I've felt all day still persists. I ate with Jung, but we conversed very little. In contrast, I spoke a great deal with Mme. Froebe, from whom I learned a number of things I must write down someday (relative to Eranos; to van der Leeuw's death; to his rediscovery of his native land, Holland; to the Dutch rituals of the "decapitation" of tulips; etc.). I spoke much also with Wolf, a German publisher living now in New York. Ruth

Norden had passed along to him my novels translated into German, so he knows me as a writer.

At 5:30 I had a "discussion" with a group of persons who had heard my lecture. I had thought I'd be able to rest this afternoon. I undressed and went to bed. Impossible to close my eyes even for a few minutes. Between 3:00 and 3:30 I had a very interesting "waking dream" which I tried in vain to stop so I could go to sleep. It continued and returned against my wishes. I imagined myself two hours later at the "discussion" (which was to take place at Casa Eranos, on the terrace). Suddenly I saw myself speaking in Sanskrit and incapable of speaking anything else. I could see what was going on around me: Christinel and the others "stunned," Jung much interested, etc. A day passes, two days. I shed my clothes and, nearly naked, take up residence on the lakeshore in the manner of an Indian ascetic. I eat nothing but a handful of rice and do not sleep (an allusion to my lecture: that *naga* who ate only a handful of rice a day and slept scarcely any at night yet had a perfect, athletic body). Jung summons the Indologist Abegg, with whom I succeed finally in making myself understood because he speaks a little Sanskrit. I tell him my name is Narada (I had related the myth of Narada in my lecture). I see how Ascona becomes the center of worldwide attention: thousands of reporters, motion picture photographers, etc. The police who come to guard Casa Gabriella, the distress of Christinel and my friends. Tucci comes by plane, and then Dasgupta, very proud that his former pupil has become famous. Sometimes I walk on the surface of the lake as if it were dry ground. I perform other yogic "miracles": kindling fire with a gesture, climbing a rope and disappearing, flying through the air, etc. The Church begins to be disturbed about my "case." I recognize no one. I live like a perfect yogin on the lakeshore. In my discussion with Dasgupta, I complain that I don't know what catastrophe has made me incapable of sleeping and eating. Then, after fifteen days, I go to sleep—and suddenly I wake up, seeking Christinel and feeling very much embarrassed to be late for Jung's lecture (which will take place tomorrow).

This waking dream "controlled" me with a mysterious power for half an hour. I want to note these details also: it was not an entirely "exalted" vision: I saw many amusing and grotesque things (the chauffeur Mario who defended the house from reporters, Mme. Froebe who acquired the manner of a high priestess of a new religion, Dasgupta's pomposity, etc.). While the dream lasted, I knew Sanskrit again very well. I heard myself speaking in Sanskrit—something I've been incapable of doing since 1932. I heard real, correct sentences, not simply words or meaningless sounds. I saw myself writing a whole notebook in Sanskrit—which was deciphered first by Abegg and then by Tucci.

At any rate, the fact that I still don't feel tired in the least makes me wonder. In any other circumstances, after eighteen or twenty hours without sleep, I'd have begun to feel a reaction. But I'm very lucid, as if I'd taken some "pep pills" (once in Portugal I took two such pills, but today I feel infinitely more "keyed up" than then). I wonder whether, in thinking about yogic processes for abolishing time, I may not have "quickened" some "image" which provoked this euphoria and this "emergence" from time never before experienced.

28 August

I recount my dream to Jung, after having related it to two other Jungian psychoanalysts (one of whom explained the whole dream by telling me I was suffering from the "Narada complex"). Jung seems very interested. His explanation: the man of science in me had succeeded in "killing" that which was real and vital in my interest for India. My dream has brought me back to reality again. Etcetera—and an etcetera which doesn't seem too interesting to me.

HERGISWILL, *30–31 August*

We are guests of Dr. Godel at Hergiswill, ten kilometers from Lucerne, in an excellent hotel on the lakeshore. In the afternoon, a concert at the Hofkirche: Bach, Pergolesi, Purcell. Then we visit the city. The excitement that comes over me every time I return to German landscapes and towns. . . . Why?

* * *

Richard Wagner's house at Tribchen. The old woman who sells us the admission tickets is careful to call our attention to the rule against playing the piano in the master's workroom. Terrible paintings inspired by Wagnerian works: Siegfried sprawled under a tree, the Rhine nymphs (and what an amusing analysis a Freudian would make of the enormous fish swimming between the legs of one nymph!), Wotan kissing the Valkyrie.

* * *

The wall of the old city, and the tower. The tavern where we take tea. A discussion about the blisses of alpinism. Dr. Godel has read a whole library on the subject recently. He shows me fascinating texts: the mountain, the high altitude considered by alpinists as Absolute Reality, sacred, "eternal." Under the pens of alpinists, terms from mystical experience recur: "eternity," "immaculate," "self-forgetfulness," etc. Some claim that the inaccessible heights are populated by *presences*. Hierophanies, as I call them.

* * *

Dr. Godel shows me a book: *La Montagne n'a pas voulu* [The Mountain Did Not So Will], in which are stories of an impressive number of accidents (falls from 800 meters, etc.) from which alpinists have nevertheless emerged unscathed. Impossible to explain except as miracles: the mountain did not will it, or the mountain saved them.

LUCERNE, *1 September*

Bach's Mass in B Minor, directed by Karaiani. Elated. Many "revelations," beginning with that sensational "Et homo factus est"!

GENEVA, *2 September*

With Roger and Alice Godel, in their car, we ascend to Jaun Pass, then go on to Château de Gruyère, and take lunch at Vevey, right on the shore of the lake. I was here in 1927. Astonished, depressed to discover suddenly that *I no longer remember anything* about that time.

Invited to dinner in Geneva this evening by Charles Baudoin. I met him last year at Fontainebleau, but I don't believe we conversed then.

3 September

Impossible to remember now where I stayed twenty-four years ago when I spent a whole summer in Geneva. I had a scholarship from the League of Nations. I continued writing "Itinerariu spiritual" for *Cu-vântul,* and I discovered *Amiel.* All I know now is that I read a great deal in the parks and the gardens of the university, which I now behold again.

* * *

This afternoon, at Café Casanova, a meeting with Corbin and Denis de Rougemont. The latter tells me that since his return from India he has immersed himself in my books. He asks me to write an article for the "secular press," setting out from my observations in the last chapter of *Le Mythe de l'éternal retour.*

PARIS, *8 September*

Glancing through *Le Figaro littéraire,* I learn of the death of Antoine Bibescu. Suddenly moved; through Antoine I preserved—in a strange way, at that—a contact with Romania and especially with Mihail Sebastian and his group. I saw him for the last time this spring, at a luncheon on rue de la Tour. He seemed quite as scatterbrained, jovial, and amusing as ever. Gouillard told me later that he had aged frightfully, that he was failing. He didn't want to talk about death, a will, or anything that might remind him of the inevitable. He did not believe in a soul or in any sort of afterlife, and yet he was terribly afraid of death.

15 September

I take up the novel again. After rereading all I wrote at Guétary, I'm not discouraged. Aside from short passages, I believe the text is "definitive." But I am seized with a kind of fury to condense, to purify the prose, to distill it to the maximum. It makes me happy whenever I can cut out a line. An adjective abolished delights me. I'm working especially on the Vădastra episodes (the only ones that seem to me perfected), and I suppress, summarize, compress.

But I haven't yet written the beginning of the novel (the "pro-logue"). The pages from Guétary don't satisfy me.

17 September

Today, for the first time, I had the sentiment that I could finish the novel, that what remains to be written is not so much that I couldn't finish it in five or six months of work. It will be necessary, however, to postpone again the lectures at the University of Lund and hold them, say, in April, and to hold those at Rome in May.

18 September

I continue the novel. Have finished integrating the Vădastra episode (the finale: Vădastra as lieutenant). I begin the Ciuc period, and I must condense to the maximum, because I was horrified today when I counted the pages of the manuscript; at this point I have already 100 pages more than were in the 1949 version. And in the fall of 1949 I proposed reducing those 380 pages of typescript to a maximum of 300!

25 September

Today I finished writing the episode at Ciuc. Ştefan Viziru is a real "neuter." Moreover, he's obsessed by his own inner discoveries. The whole life and atmosphere of the prison camp are seen from outside by someone who has neither the time nor the intention to see it. I believe I've succeeded in writing a good chapter. But I haven't included here any of my own experiences at Ciuc. I shall have to use them on another occasion. Ştefan might meet someone in Paris in 1945 who will evoke them—but Ştefan won't remember, because he didn't "see" them.

26 September

Last night, in order to refresh my memory on certain passages in *Et nunc. . .* , I took down Gide's *Journal* again. How many pages written not because he felt a need to record something strictly personal just for himself but as fragments or notes for studies, essays, or dialogues! The same is true of many pages of Green's *Journal*. Aside from intimacies which Green suppresses (at least for the time being), one senses that his journal satisfied his need for writing. The man filled several pages every day. He was freer here than he was with the manuscript of his novel; he could be fragmentary, personal, allusive. Green didn't write articles; all that was not confiscated by the novel passed over into the journal. That is what makes it, in the final analysis, so interesting and valid. Like a notebook, a *fragmentarium*.

28 September

Every afternoon and sometimes in the mornings, I come to work here, in Sibylle's ceramics studio at 47 rue Saint-Ouen. I leave home with the novel manuscript in a briefcase. It takes ten or twelve minutes to walk from rue Duhesme to rue Saint-Ouen, exactly the amount of time I need to "get into" the novel—that is, to get out of the agitated atmosphere of the house (because everyone is back from vacation now). On Saint-Ouen, next to the ceramics studio, is Sibylle's room. A large wooden table by the window. I see the tops of the plane trees and hear the noise of the street. The building is an old hotel abandoned and half destroyed during the war. Several poor families have moved into the ruins, including an Italian family with a host of children whom I sometimes encounter on the stairs. The entrance, through an archway, is gloomy, and the stairs are of wood. But I've gotten used to these things, and I like it here because I have the feeling that there's no one near me, that the building is empty. The terrible din of the street I do not hear.

30 September

Interrupting work on the novel for a few minutes today, I try to make a connection between literary art and the conclusions I've reached in my studies of archaic mentality. The images and archetypes (i.e., that which is ahistorical, suprapersonal, "eternal" in man) correspond, on the plane of the novel, to that which you find in any character if you "analyze" him, if you concern yourself with his "interior life." Drama, novelty, originality—you meet these exclusively in the events in which he is involved. Thus, it is useless to "analyze" a character when he is doing something out of the ordinary: you will find the same images, the same archetypes you have found in every other character in a similar situation. Simply tell *what he is doing!* This is his "novelty," his originality, his authenticity—what he *does,* not what he *thinks as he acts.* Every other character would "think" (more precisely, would let his mind function) exactly as he.

What I have just written is very confused and approximate. If I were to be more specific, I'd lose too much time and, above all, I'd leave the atmosphere of the novel. But I observe that I've reached this conclusion through an inner necessity while writing the novel: Ştefan (as well as the other main characters), as soon as he "acts," properly speaking, as soon as he becomes a creator of events, ceases (in my consciousness as a writer) to exist as an interior reality; I see him then exclusively *externally,* acting. I asked myself today why I see him this way, and I wrote this note. But I shall have to return to this matter at greater length when I no longer have the manuscript of the novel facing me.*

4 October

I was able to write only one page all afternoon yesterday. Today I didn't accomplish even that much. I don't "believe" in the novel any more; I've become detached from it. I look at the characters as I have seen them up to now and as I know they will behave from here on in the hundreds of pages that still remain to be written—and they no longer interest me. I must stop working on the novel. Besides, there are numerous other urgent things I need to do: the studies on yoga for the American volume edited by Sorokin, the article for *Journal de psychologie,* the revision of the text for the *Eranos-Jahrbuch,* etc.

7 October

Yet, in spite of everything, I haven't stopped. I worked both yesterday and the day before, recasting, augmenting, and deepening a scene which seemed to me too summarily written (Biriş-Ştefan, 1939). I discovered a great many new things about Biriş: his tuberculosis imbued with memories from adolescence, his sense of humor which until now I saw only on the plane of the irony of an intellectual. He begins to acquire dimensions of his own, apart from his pedantry.

The difficulty of which Partenie will complain in his private journal (the journal Ştefan will read in Paris in 1948): that it is so hard to write a novel with "intellectual" characters because all intellectuals are alike, speak the same language, have the same psychology, etc.—this difficulty is, in the first place, my own. I sense it overwhelmingly

---

*I don't believe I ever returned to it.

sometimes, especially in the case of Ştefan. When I throw him into dramatic or somewhat absurd scenes, I *sense* him rather concretely. But when he "becomes himself" again, he escapes me, because then he is a simple intellectual, like all of us.

10 October

For a week the sky has been clear, a pale, smoky blue, and every morning the same temptation arises to go down into the city, to reach the banks of the Seine as soon as possible, to return to Saint-Germain-des Prés. Sometimes, in the afternoons, I go out for a walk. I stop at the old bookstands along the Seine, something I haven't done for several years. But I resist as much as I can. That time, however melancholic, however beatific it may be, also passes. I sense it flowing, as though through my fingers, in my bloodstream. I don't know how much longer this mood for novel writing will last. I keep telling myself that I must make the most of this period of good literary disposition, which began on 15 September and which I shall have to interrupt soon anyhow, in order to finish the texts promised for October. I'm still at the same chapter which features Biriş as the central character and which gives me so much to do because the action extends over a full year (March 1939 to March 1940)—and what a year! I am progressing, however, at the rate of three pages per day. I don't want to stop before finishing this chapter.

21 October

The novel was interrupted a week ago. I've put the final touches to the Eranos lecture which will figure also in the volume *Images et symboles*. For several days I've been reading much in Russian. Have been reading about Russia as well, about the "protohistory" and history of the Revolution. I have understood once again what a temptation for a "creator"—someone who feels and knows he has something to say—are "the people," the struggle for the "good of society," revolution, etc. It is rather easy to resist vulgar, brutally selfish temptations—for instance, the temptation to make yourself rich by shutting your eyes, living an agreeable life, and upsetting no one. Much harder is it to resist the appeal of great social ideals. "How can I study the problem of the polar ice cap when there's so much misery all around me?'' Kropotkin exclaimed. Only with difficulty can you resist the temptation to give yourself to great ideals, because the appeal is directed toward *that which is best in you,* toward that which is most human, most deep.

And yet, you *must* resist! If you want to *make* something, you must resist even sublime urges, temptations to give yourself in sacrifice (as a true *narodnik,* or revolutionary). For a ''creator,'' the road that leads to others resembles the road taken by prophets, saints, reformers, and spiritual masters of the type of Socrates or Milarepa.

10 November

Have been reading Russian all the time. But I must begin to speak it too. I observe that I always get the accent wrong. The language pleases me more and more. I'll be happy when I can read the great poets without difficulty.

12 November

I reread *Aventura spirituală.* Disappointed. The play is ''frankly bad.'' When I recall the good opinion I had of it at the time I was writing it, I shudder. Is it possible for an author to be so utterly mistaken? The theme still interests me, but I'd have to rework the play from the first page to the last. It must be written in a different tone. Will I ever find the time to do it? Is it worth doing over?

22 November

I awoke this morning with a harsh, brilliant sun shining in my face. It is cold, the sky is blue, quite clear, and yet a light fog hovers as usual over Paris. I set out for Sacré-Coeur, going up rue des Saules, as I do each day, past the Lapin Agile and the vineyards of Montmartre, turning at rue Cortot and entering the cathedral through the Pilgrim's Gate. I climbed slowly, my spirits rising as I went; and more and more tumultuously I sensed in my soul this revelation: our exile from the homeland is a long and difficult initiatory ordeal, destined to purify and transform us. The distant, inaccessible country will be like a paradise to which we return spiritually, that is, "in spirit," in secret, but *really*. I have thought much of Dante and his exile. It makes no difference whether we ever return, physically, to the homeland. And we must not torment ourselves asking what country or what sort of people we will find there on our return. Dante's Florence was no longer medieval Florence, just as the city that came later, the Florence of the Renaissance, did not last long. Political autonomy was lost to the benefit of Italy, which was born later. And today Italy itself will abandon its own autonomy for a new and larger political integration. But all these things have not been able to abolish Dante's "patria." A "fatherland" like that was revealed to me today, as I was ascending rue des Saules, with Sacré-Coeur on my left looking like a recently whitewashed St. Sofia, too white and too clean against the deep-blue sky. A fatherland like that—but we shall have to become like Dante (not, of course, in his genius, in his grandeur, but in his spiritual situation). As I wrote to Vintilă Horia, we must take Dante as our model, not Ovid.

24 November

At Andrée Chedide's place. I meet Raymond de Vergnas, professor of English literature at the Sorbonne, who has recently published a novel, *Le millième jour*. I tell him that I admire his courage: professor *and* novelist. He confides in me that R.M., who might have had the chance, will never become a professor at the Sorbonne because of the "scandal" his novel provoked. In the case of E., it's a different story (the truth is, E.'s novel seems terrible). But I didn't intend to write about these things. A long and animated discussion on the novel. I maintain, as on so many other occasions, the "irreplaceability" of the narrative novel, the so-called novel-novel, which fills the place of myths for the modern world. I observe how intently they are listening to me, as certain others have listened before. And all at once I have the feeling that something is wrong: these things "pass into the public domain," they are accepted and assimilated before being given an identity, before being presented in a coherent form, before being published. I realize once again that I talk too much. It is imprudent.

1 December

I continue the work, but with only a quarter of my strength. A new attack of "vagotonia" for several days. Am detached from *Images et symboles,* although the book is almost finished; I'd have only to write a conclusion. But maybe it's in my destiny to "dash off" the endings of all my books. Brice Parain, seeing he couldn't convince me to rework and develop the last chapter of *Le Mythe de l'éternel retour,* told me: "Never mind; it will be a book with an abrupt ending, like Stendhal's novels."

The conclusion to *Images et symboles* could be a point of departure for a philosophy of culture and a theology of history.

8 December

Two days before his death, Gide told his doctor, Jean Delay: "J'ai peur que mes phrases ne deviennent grammaticalement inexactes" [I have a fear of my phrases becoming grammatically incorrect]. Gide's continuing obsession not to "diminish," not to become "agraphic." Nothing matters to him on the eve of his demise except that which might affect his mental integrity and language. The supreme "existential" homage which he renders to precise language and clear expression. I wonder whether, indeed, he didn't think about anything else, whether death was for him nothing more than an ordinary "end." What had become of his passionate youth? I imagine myself in his situation: I believe I would be unable to think of grammar, or of graphia or agraphia; at any rate, I believe I'd be thinking of *something else.*

Also, his passion to carry constantly a pocket notebook, to write anywhere, anything, and to read and reread it until the eve of his death. "Le journal jusqu'à la mort"—so Georges Bataille entitles his article [on Gide] in *Critique.* What more would he have said?

10 December

An enthusiastic letter from C. Baudouin, to whom I sent copies of both *Le Mythe* and *Traité* in early September. He sends me also an excerpt from his journal, written at age nineteen, in which he relates an experience which, he declares, he has come to understand only now, after reading my books. The excerpt is quite interesting: an experience of a fundamental renewal in which all the mythic elements of the periodic repetition of the cosmogony are present. "I understand now that I was visited by the archetype of the regeneration of time. Nothing is missing: the date of the equinox, the abolition of past time, the allusion (as if by chance!) to the 'eternal return,' and even the deluge in the form of a storm and a diluvial downpour."

The pages from his journal are very exciting, indeed. I wonder whether I ought to publish them in a new edition of *Le Mythe*, in an appendix, together with a few other notes and documents.

12 December

Yesterday afternoon I was working at transcribing the final pages of conclusions to *Images et symboles* when I received a visit from Jean Pierre Meister, an advisor at the Swiss legation in Buenos Aires, who brought me news and gifts from Giza. We talked for two hours—I on pins and needles. I *had* to finish the conclusions by 7:00 P.M., in order to be able to take these last pages to Gouillard for him to correct. And after Meister's departure, I spread things out to write and transcribe. The last page I wrote without making a rough draft, looking at my watch the whole time! Thus I conclude a book I've thought about for ten years! When I returned from Gouillard's, I was seized with remorse. I intend to review this text, to improve it and complete it in the galley proofs.

MONTE CARLO, *27 December*

We have been here since 22 December, at Hôtel Excelsior. The day after we arrived, the weather turned bad. I don't feel like doing anything. I read several of Faulkner's novels with the same admiration as always for his unlimited literary craft.

An uneventful Christmas: loneliness, boredom. If only I could get started again on the novel. But I still have to write a preface for the posthumous book of Paul Vulliaud, *La Fin du monde,* and the article promised for *Preuves.* Moreover, I haven't any place to write. The walls here are thinner than those at Hôtel de Suède. The neighbors on the left, an old woman and her grandson, exasperate me. They stay home all day. They rise at 7:00 A.M. and immediately begin talking loudly and harshly, as though taking turns giving orders to a regiment.

I arranged with the manager to work in a room next to his office, in the lobby area. The noise is terrific there also. Telephones, the kitchen, voices in the lobby. I'm very discouraged, almost depressed. The hotel is exceptionally inexpensive; if we move, it will cost us twice as much. On the other hand, I have to work! I have only two free months ahead to devote to the novel.

Undated, 1951

Le Nuit bengali has passed almost unnoticed, and I wonder whether it's not better this way, i.e., whether a success with the press and the public might not have put me in a false light: because the novel represents only one aspect of my literary oeuvre, and not even the most significant one. It would not be convenient for me to be *identified* as the author of *this* novel (even after it was "enobled" both by G. Bachelard's characterization of it as "une mythologie de la volupté" and by the testimonies of Tucci, Renou, and other orientalists that, at last, something of the authentic contemporary India has been reflected in a European literary work).

More important, one could say that this lack of success is due to circumstances. Indeed, a little while after its appearance, Marcel Brion announced at the end of his "Chronicle of Foreign Books" in *Le Monde* that, in the following week, he would discuss "le beau roman de Mircea Eliade." For a foreign writer, one could not imagine a more prestigious "launching." But the column in *Le Monde* has never appeared. Marcel Brion explained to me, in an overly friendly letter, that four typed pages would not have been enough, that he needed twelve or fifteen, and that therefore he would write a study for *Revue des deux mondes*. Up to the present day, that study has not appeared, and I don't believe it ever will.* I'm sure something intervened, but I don't know what. Probably some slander was lodged with the directors of *Le Monde;* it matters little

---

*I was not mistaken (1971).

from what source (it could have come equally as well from the legation or from some "comrade in exile"). But there is no room for doubt that this mishap has buried the book. In those weeks of late autumn, the nonappearance of Marcel's chronicle amounted to a catastrophe, not only from a financial point of view but especially because the failure of *La Nuit bengali* annuls the possibility of seeing other novels translated.

But now I tell myself that the author of my denunciation has, quite unintentionally, done me a great service. It is *not appropriate* that I should be discovered as a writer *today* through a novel written at age twenty-five. If it is destined for me to become known as a novelist here in Western Europe, it would be more natural to be discovered through my work of maturity, that is, *Noaptea de Sânziene*. Only such a book—in the event that it will have the luck to be read by a hundred or two hundred readers and critics whose opinion I respect—will suffice to *save,* that is, to reveal the significance of all the Romanian efforts that preceded it.

MONTE CARLO, *2 January 1952*

Only during the past few hours have I had a room that is truly *mine,* where I'll be able to work undisturbed by neighbors. I changed rooms several times before getting this one. At a certain moment, I found this room—a room without neighbors but also without light, in which the bulb burns all day. Formerly a storage room. . . . To come to the Côte d'Azur and write by artificial light, as in a tower of a medieval prison!

I have written a very "so-so" preface for Vuillaud's book. I know, I know, I'm making a mockery of myself, of my scientific "authority," but there's nothing to be done: in order to regain my freedom, I sacrifice whatever I put my hand to. Yesterday I began "Examen leprosorum" for *Preuves.* I've dreamed of this article for a year. But I have to dispatch the text by 5 January.

4 January

I finish writing "Examen leprosorum." Christinel types it, and I post it in the evening mail. I begin immediately to reread the manuscript of the novel. I start at chapter 3, which only half satisfies me.

5 *January*

Today I begin correcting chapter 1. I rewrite, simplify, and add a few pages. Nevertheless, it's hard to make progress. The same difficulty: Ştefan's terrible ambiguity. I don't know how to present him *at the beginning.*

In the evening I continue, with an effort, the reading of Faulkner's *The Sound and the Fury.* Of all his books I've read, this is, in my opinion, the least successful. A dated technique: 1930, influences of James Joyce, John dos Passos. What is the point of that long, absurd, uninteresting interior monologue of a neurotic on the verge of suicide? The pretentious facility of the interior monologue, which gives you the false sense of authenticity! I know all too well the attractions, pitfalls, and falsity of the interior monologue and the mental film: I utilized them in *Lumina ce se stinge* (in that very year, 1930!). But where can such a procedure lead? To the kabbalistic universe of the latter James Joyce: the cipher; the mystic solidarity among sounds, spaces, and lights; multidimensional, seminal universes. I must write a long article, which could be entitled ''On the Necessity for the 'Novel-Novel,' '' showing the autonomous, glorious, irreducible dimension of *narration,* the formula of myth and mythology readapted to the modern consciousness. Showing that modern man, like the man of archaic societies, cannot exist without myths, without exemplary stories. The metaphysical dignity of narrative—ignored, to be sure, by generations of realists and ''psychologizers,'' who began by raising to the first rank psychological analysis, then spectral analysis, arriving finally at facile formulas for filming psychomental phenomena. The great lesson of several Anglo-Saxon writers (Thornton Wilder, Faulkner in his short stories, but also Graham Greene), rehabilitating direct narration, showing how metaphysics and theology can be revealed by narration as such, rather than by commentaries or analyses by the author.

Besides, it seems to me that Faulkner himself renounced the interior monologue. *Sanctuary, Light in August*—clearly superior to this *The Sound and the Fury,* in which I progress with so much reluctance.

11 January

Today there is a storm on the sea. Gray billows, whitecapped. Am suddenly reminded of the winter spent at Cascaes.

In the past several days I have worked on the novel with considerable enthusiasm and profit. I reread, corrected, and augmented chapters 2–5. I am now up to the London episodes, which seemed among the few valid ones in the first version. I was mistaken here too. They're written too loosely; they're dry and superficial. Apart from the short scenes with Vădastra and Antim, the rest must be redone in toto.

Until evening the day was clear and cold. It was a pity to stay shut up in my room all day. But I have the feeling that if I don't "advance" the novel this time, I'll abandon it altogether. And the great difficulty still remains *Time*. I proposed in the beginning, in 1949, to write in such a way that one could sense the flow of time. But to do that I'd have to extend the book to two thousand pages. I am obliged, therefore, to "jump," to concentrate; but I keep asking myself whether the prose will still have the "bulk," the density it would have had if I had allowed time to "flow."

16 January

Only today did I finish correcting chapter 7 (London) and some pages that still seemed to falter in chapter 6. Thus I find myself, on the trajectory of the narrative, exactly at the point I had reached in August 1949 at Capri. I can say that in a sense I've written a new novel. Only two long chapters to do, and I shall have finished part 1. A good share of this material was written during the fall of 1949. However, I doubt whether I can save more than ten or fifteen pages. I shall have to resort more and more insistently to the technique of *Huliganii* (mental film, short synchronic chapters, etc.) in order to be able to concentrate the action of the year 1941. Having renounced my absurd ambition to write a "fresco," I'm no longer obsessed by the great historical events (the declaration of war, etc.). All these things, if I live, will find their place in *Viaţă nouă*.

21 January

I work on the novel, apparently, all day—but effectively for just a few hours. This is not a period of "inspiration" for me. I write slowly, stopping several times on every page. Progress is difficult. The second part, however, I "see" articulated with increasing clarity. Am in the middle of chapter 8 now. Part 1 will have nine chapters. In file folders I keep finding texts written two years ago, but only rarely can I use them. Not only are they poorly written, but their narrative substance is lacking in interest. The novel must continually be reinvented. If I had understood that fact last summer, and if I hadn't labored to "save" parts of the old versions already typed, I'd be much farther along today.

25 January

I finish chapter 8. Am satisfied that at least I succeeded in changing Stella Zissu, so pale and insipid in the first version, and in introducing Irina's family. But I'm still just as dissatisfied as ever with Ioana. I hope Ioana will acquire relief in part 2, at the premonition of her death, and, after that, in the recollections of Ştefan and Irina.

31 January

When I came here to Monte Carlo I told myself that the month of January would suffice for me to finish part 1 and begin part 2. On this last day of January, I find myself scarcely at the middle of chapter 9. And still I haven't written the prologue.

Two days with Alice Godel, who arrived by plane from Isma'ilia. She brings me the doctor's manuscript, *Essai sur l'expérience libératrice,* which is to be published, by Gallimard, with a preface I am to write. Masui is pressing me for the chapters on yoga, for the American edition edited by Sorokin. I have an immense backlog of correspondence and several articles to write, plus the preface for V. Bumbeşti's novel.

2 February

Today, at noon, I finished part 1. I still don't dare reread it. Nevertheless, I'm satisfied, enthused. The final scene I saw in 1949, and it seemed too familiar, too many times filmed mentally for me to be able to write it with the freshness which alone could "save" it, make it plausible.

9 February

I have finished, finally, the "prologue." I believe that in this week alone I wrote four or five versions—in addition to those numerous other efforts of last summer which no longer satisfied me. Tremendous difficulty with the "atmosphere": I had to avoid at all costs the "faery" or fantastic air of *Şarpele,* yet without sacrificing the imponderable, absurd, "predestined" element which was implied (more precisely, camouflaged) in "the car that was to have disappeared at midnight" and which in any case I couldn't discard. Destiny, time, revelations of a supernatural order—all are "shown" in my novel through the presence, more or less real, of a car. "Ileana's car" means, for Ştefan, the presentiment of a time and an existence when *they will be together* without sacrificing Ioana. He could not imagine during 1936 and the years following that Ioana would be killed in the air raid of 4 April 1944 and that he could *be with Ileana* yet without losing the love of Ioana.

18 February

In a letter from Brutus Coste, I learn that Anton Golopenţia has died. He had been in prison for two years. One day his wife was called to the morgue to identify the body. He was the last person I expected to die—like that, in prison. I remember the summer of 1946, on rue des Saints-Pères, when Anton came to my place repeatedly and met with Brutus and Titus Pogoneanu. His terrible lucidity, his self-control, and his sadness. He told Cioran once that if he were not married, he'd commit suicide. He spoke of a "lamasary" somewhere in the Car-pathians. He dreamed, without any hope, of a house in the mountains where "technicians" could gather and work.

I remember meeting him once in Munich in 1937. He was the first to tell me about Jaspers's *Philosophie.* Anton could not "believe," although he understood religion and the sociology of religion very well. His sadness always frightened me. He spoke little, and his speech was condensed and picturesque. I regretted later that we hadn't become friends, that our meetings were so sporadic. In that same summer of

1937 he said to me at Munich: "Times are going to get harder and harder. For us Romanians a single problem is posed: how to hibernate, how to hide within ourselves and let the winter pass over us."

                              * * *

For several days, a new attack of "vagotonia." Have written a rather ordinary preface to Roger Godel's *Essai*. Now I'm struggling with the studies for Sorokin. But I'm not "inspired." My mind is still on "literature." Moreover, after having worked on the novel for the past six weeks, writing in French is "hard going" now. (Cioran tells me that on a day when he reads a German book he can't write good French.)

PARIS, *1 March*

We returned the day before yesterday, after dark. How I envy those who know how to keep a journal! Men who find time to record impressions daily, no matter how tired or bored they may be. So many observations, happenings, plans—for the past two weeks, the past year, it's all the same—which I didn't record and have begun to forget already!

I've had neither the desire nor the time to start part 2 of the novel. Ten days have been lost waiting for comments from the first readers: Spaltmann, Vona, and Monica Lovinescu. I received them only today. From Vona's letter I couldn't tell whether the novel is a success.

In my letter of response to Spaltmann today, I make several general observations about the novel that are not devoid of interest. In writing to him I discover the deep meaning of Ştefan's "behavior" in the final scene of part 1.

13 March

For ten days ill: "vagotonia," complicated by gastritis (or possibly an ulcer; an X-ray will decide). Weak, dizzy, drowsy, I can barely write urgent articles and a few letters. I still haven't prepared the Musée Guimet lectures to be given three days from now, to say nothing of my course for the University of Lund.

Encouraging comments from the first readers, especially Vona, Monica, and Virgil Ierunca. This last, enthusiastic about Ştefan and the ending of part 1 (but not interested in Vădastra, who seems to him simply a successful "epic" figure, devoid of "signs"). He asks me repeatedly: "But can it be true that Ştefan and Ileana will *never* meet again in *this world?*"

20 March

Roger Martin du Gard, on Gide's method of writing novels (*Les Faux Monnayeurs*): "He refused to adhere to a preestablished plan. He did not know himself where he was going, nor did he know very clearly where he wanted to go. He wrote by impulse, according to the caprice of the moment. In the middle of a chapter, in order to strengthen a scene, sometimes simply to make a savory rejoinder, he would invent a new character, someone he had never dreamed of before, whose silhouette is suddenly sketched and tempts him but who will never do anything in the story, who will not even find a role to play."

It is as though I myself were describing my own unfortunate "method" of novel writing. I began *Noaptea de Sânziene* knowing only this much: that Ştefan would love two women and that he would spend his life trying to understand the mystery possibly camouflaged in this circumstance, trying above all to assume this situation in the hope that "something will be revealed to him" and that he will in this way obtain another method of existence (full and glorious). The characters appear haphazardly. Biriş appeared in order to propound a theory. (I refer to the first version, in which Biriş, like all the others, does nothing but talk.) Doamna Porumbache, I remember very well, I invented in order to get out of a pointless scene with Ştefan and Biriş: they were having a discussion, chatting idly, and all at once I became bored and d-na Porumbache appeared! She knocked on the door and came in with a tray of coffee and sweets. Cătălina I invented because I had led Ştefan and Biriş into meeting each other on the street, and I was afraid they would embark again on a terrible discussion of Time and History. A way out had to be found: Mişu Weissmann appeared on the sidewalk in front of them, but he was not alone (had he been alone, there was danger that the discussion would break out anew), for Cătălina was with him. I knew nothing about her! Fortunately, Biriş told Ştefan that she was Bibicescu's girlfriend, and then I understood. (I understood then also that he loved her too. But why hadn't he told me that before?) Bibicescu, in turn, was invented through a mix-up over initials. In the first version, I didn't know the names of the characters yet, so I indicated them by initials. Biriş at first was B., but because I felt he talked too much I distributed part of his speeches to another character whom I still hadn't seen. I indicated him in the manuscript as "Bib." at the places where B. no longer was to exist. But since I wrote quickly and poorly, B., Bib., and Bir. became confused, and, in the process of transcribing, some of Bibicescu's responses reverted to Biriş again, and vice versa.

Only beginning with part 2 can I say that I know what I want; I know at least in broad outline what will happen and the order in which things will occur.

24 March

Despite the regimen, despite all the medicines and bismuth I've taken in the past two weeks (almost) since I saw Dr. Hunwald, I feel ill all the time, weak, exhausted. I have to have a blood count of the red cells and a stomach X-ray taken. I don't understand what's wrong. An ulcer? Cancer?

* * *

Yesterday I was at Jacques Masui's place. He showed me a photograph of Varille. What a strange head, what a bulging forehead, as though it were ready to tip over, to fall out!

Someone remarked about the mysterious deaths in the past few years: all those who, among other things, were concerned with symbolism and archaic or oriental traditions, from Coomaraswamy to Varille. I amuse myself thinking about how I twice have postponed the trip to Sweden (in November and in March) and that I'll be traveling both ways by airplane. It could be, it could be. . . . I'd regret most of all leaving the novel unfinished.

29 March

I visited Germany for the first time in 1934. I went only to Berlin—in fact, only to the Stadtbibliothek; I was putting the final touches to *Yoga*. On the train, returning to Romania on a clear, golden

September day, I "saw" a novel: two people fall in love in the prime of their youth (about 1910–12); both get married to other partners more or less resignedly, they have children, etc.; then at age forty or forty-five they become free again, they meet and find anew the love and bliss they lost in youth. In the meantime, the war has occurred, the reunification of Romania, and all that followed.

Now as I think of it, *Noaptea de Sânziene* as I "saw" it in June 1949 is the same novel as that of 1934, except that the story begins two and a half decades later. The fundamental problem remains: the meeting again after a long period of time. Interjected into this plot, of course, is Ștefan's love for two women (the theme of *Întoarcerea din rai*). From there on, the novel has kept changing as the writing has progressed.

5 April

Conversation with Dr. Claudian. I hadn't seen him for two years. He tells me many things, but this story moves me most:

A small, frail Legionary comes to him, begging: "Make me well, *domnule* doctor; I've got to leave soon. I'm parachuting into Romania. I've jumped twice before, in 1941 and 1945." He tells him the story of his life. "My mother raised me by begging with her knapsack. I became a lycée teacher, but I couldn't help her, because I joined the Legion. They put me in prison; I fled the country. Last year someone came from my village and told me mother had died. Still poor, still begging. On her death bed she said, 'My son—he's with his buddies. He doesn't know I've been begging with my knapsack.' "

The man was sure his mother hadn't said this in anger, that she hadn't reproached him. But on hearing it, his heart broke. He has to return to his village, to go and pray at his mother's grave. He found out that men are being parachuted into Romania, and since he had jumped twice before he wants to offer himself at the "office" where parachutists are engaged. But for this he must first be cured of his illness. "Make me well, *domnule* doctor! Make me well quickly!"

6 April

I come across this extraordinary notation of Victor Hugo: "La nature, qui met sur l'invisible le masque du visible, est une apparence corrigée par un transparence" [Nature, which puts on the invisible the mask of the visible, is an appearance corrected through a transparency].

In a sense, that formula anticipates the whole metaphysics latent in *Noaptea de Sânziene*.

ASCONA, 5 June

I reopen this notebook on a cloudy morning. We are at Ascona, in Casa Gabriella, guests of Olga Froebe for a month. We arrived three days ago; since then I've done nothing but doze in the chaise longue on the terrace, with a book in my hand. I came here with the intention of taking up the novel again. But as yet I haven't been "seized" by literature. On the contrary, in this *Archiv für Symbolforschung* I feel myself tempted by my old passions.

I have reopened this notebook in order to record a few dates: the trips to Sweden and Italy, the reunion with Papini. In the waiting room at the Copenhagen airport I jotted down a number of impressions, but it seems childish to copy them here. Two lectures at Lund, 22 and 23 April, in the hall where Ehnmark holds his courses at the university. On shamanism. Introduced by Ehnmark. At the second lecture the dean thanked me, reading from a little piece of paper he couldn't decipher. (Dinner at the dean's; impromptu lecture on Yoga, which I had to give at the insistence of Madame Holberg.) Seminars on Romanian philology with Alf Lombard and two doctoral candidates, each session lasting two hours. Wikander in the hospital. Just before dinner, an hour spent with him, talking. He still doesn't know what's wrong with him—a gastric ulcer? (He's afraid of cancer.) Vertigo and hemorrhages. Meeting with Martin Nilsson. He gives me several books and sells me one at a forty-percent discount, as for bookstores. "You may pay me," he says. Fortunately, I had exchanged some currency.

The Lund Cathedral—and the clock. I stayed at Hotel Temperance, located between two undertaking establishments. Everytime I returned home, I stole a glance at the window of the first place: funerary urns, examples of inscriptions, flowers of stone.

Automobile trips at different times to Malmö, Lands-Krona, Hälsingborg. Also the village of Viken with its ancient houses and its shabby beach on the warmer shore of the sea. The house of the (honorary) Romanian consul at Malmö, full of pistols. Forced to drink all evening. And the next morning I had to get up at 7:00 to catch the train to Malmö in order to reach the airport in time for my flight to Paris. A feeling of great calm and peace returned to me on the airplane. To that flight at six thousand feet many things in my life will be related; I sense them already, although I don't understand them.

9 June

I've been reading all the time, having let myself be drawn into the bizarre and diverse library of Mme. Froebe. One morning I took out the manuscript of the novel, but after an hour of fruitless effort I gave it up. It didn't "go."

To note a few more items from the month of May: at Rome a lecture, "Secret Languages and Mystical Techniques," on 7 May in the auditorium of Tucci's Oriental Institute. I *sense* that it was a very great success. The mystical experience, ecstasy, as the recovery of the paradisiacal Adamic state. All these things will be developed in *Nostalgie du Paradis*. Nevertheless, before I write the book, I shall publish the text of this lecture in Tucci's series.

Saturday, 10 May, in the little conference room of the institute, an improvised talk on method in the history of religions. I speak for an hour with absolutely no notes. Interesting discussion. Dan Petraşincu, whom I had met a few days earlier, seems enthusiastic. We talk until 2:00 A.M. in the Caffe Rosatti. He tells me about mutual friends and writers in Romania. What he has to say isn't all sad; sometimes it's interesting too.

I wrote to Papini, and the next day I receive a very cordial, friendly letter *expresso*. He writes that he has never forgotten me, that he has followed my activities, that I am the Frazier of my generation, that he keeps *Traité* always near at hand. He invites me to Florence, and we

have lunch together and remain in conversation all afternoon. On
Saturday, 17 May, I went to visit him on via Guerrazzi. I had seen
him only once before, in April 1927, on via G. B. Vico. After that
visit, I wrote an interview article for *Universul literar* which, I was
told, made my colleagues in journalism and literature green with
envy. That interview "launched" me! Since then, for a quarter of a
century, I had not seen him, although I had returned to Italy several
times.

* * *

A cloudy day, with occasional intervals of slow, warm rain. I finish
rereading—ten years after the first reading—Jung and Kerényi's
Einführung in das Wesen der Mythologie.

At teatime, Mme. Froebe tells me about visions experienced by
certain eccentric guests, among them Alice Bailey, who saw a monk
repeatedly entering the window on the right (all this happened in the
room where we're staying, on the second floor, the room in which I'm
writing this). Alice Bailey (what an able adventuress! I met her in
London in 1940; my Polish translator—God only knows what her name
was; and what an intelligent, likable, informed woman!—gave me a
letter of recommendation, and Alice Bailey invited me to dinner. She
was with her husband—a nonentity—and a friend, a tremendously
voluble American woman, probably her patroness, because she paid for
the dinner. Alice Bailey conducted a school of "initiation by correspondence" with a rather high tuition; she had published a number of
books—unreadable, and absolutely worthless)—Alice Bailey evoked
her master and protector in Tibet, with whom she was in regular
communication through telepathy; and with the aid of a ritual she
expelled the shade of that mysterious monk who kept coming in the
window. After that, Mme. Froebe adds, the monk visited the room next
door, where a young Dutch Quaker was staying; he would come at 2:00
A.M. Since the young man's room was directly over Mme. Froebe's
bedroom, she would hear him jump out of bed and turn on the light. He
would start reading aloud from the Bible. I don't know what sins that
monk had committed, but on hearing the words of the Bible he would
disappear.

During the past few days, Mme. Froebe has told me a number of anecdotes about Eranos, about occultist groups in England and Switzerland, and especially about Jung. If my lack of inspiration continues, I shall try to record at least a few of them (the "Gnostic ritual" with the glass of wine and the ring, performed by Jung in 1936, through which he bound himself to her; this "ritual" I must by all means relate).

But I had started to write about my visit with Papini, and I want to continue. Three days ago I received from him a letter, forwarded from Paris, in which he complained that he had had no news for me since our meeting of 17 May and that I had not sent him the books I had promised. This morning I received here a second letter—very cordial—responding to my reply; he has read my article in *Revue de culture européenne* and is now reading *Le Mythe*.

He had written me earlier that he was nearly blind. But when he wrote the dedications for me in some of his books, I saw it for myself: he took off his glasses, leaned over with his face about two centimeters from the page, and wrote rather disjointedly, not connecting the letters to one another. Nevertheless, he told me he writes more easily than he reads. A secretary, whom I saw in one of the rooms of his library, reads to him aloud. Otherwise, he is healthy. He still has the same rich head of hair he had a quarter of a century ago (very slightly thin at the crown, but noticeable only when he bows his head). But he has lost almost all his teeth. Among the few that remain, one has grown down like a fang. He speaks French fluently, but sometimes, because of his teeth, it is difficult to understand him. Smoking he has given up (I remember how he smoked incessantly in 1927 from a large box of cigarettes which he had placed between us). When he set the empty coffee cup on the tray, he felt with his fingers for the place.

We talked for three hours: history of religions, Christianity, Orient-Occident, the historic moment, France, the "nostalgia for paradise" (I summarized my theories for him)—and he told me about the books he is writing, in particular, *Giudizio universale* (The Last Judgment). But there is no point in my writing about these matters here. I must redact that "Rencontre avec Giovanni Papini" which I promised him and promised myself (because I want to *bear witness* on behalf of this author of my adolescence). Here, I wish to note only the extraordinary, unexpected cordiality he showed me. In *Traité* he had marked a large number of pages. He asked me about the brotherhood of the demon and the saint (Verzelia and Sisinie). Is it, however, only the joy of his finding again an admirer who is today an "accomplished scientific authority" in Paris? Does he not also have the feeling that the new generations are beginning to forget him, and it pleases him, therefore, that a "scientific authority" from France is eager to talk with him? Especially from France, where he knows he has never succeeded in being recognized as a "European author."

* * *

This evening the lake is engulfed in a low fog, gray and leaden. An oppressive heat seems to have descended between the sinister mountains which are no longer visible. And the hot, humid, stifling air persists. Now and then thunder is heard, distant and indecisive. It thundered softly like that all last night, and yet only a few drops of rain fell. I'm reminded of that evening of late June last year when I met with Spaltmann and other friends at the Deux Magots. It had been torrid all day, and toward evening a storm of sorts broke out half-successfully. In the warm rain the city seemed even hotter, and the air heavy and suffocating. We all felt it—the impression of a preapocalyptic night. A sinister anticipation, with the bolts of lightning criscrossing the sky fruitlessly above the haze.

On that night I realized that all "meetings" are possible, that the simple, elementary implausibility which the real meetings in life always contain allows me to articulate all the meetings in the second part of *Noaptea de Sânziene.*

10 June

Sometimes I think about Romania and what I left there at home—manuscripts, journal, correspondence, library—and I become depressed. All those things I could lose, if indeed I haven't lost them already. Never to be able to find any of them again, to have no "souvenir," no concrete *trace* of my childhood, adolescence, and youth; to return—if I ever do—to a city in which I shall no longer find anything that once was *mine* (a letter from adolescence, a notebook with jottings, a photograph, a book I've read)—the thought horrifies me! It may well be that my whole past up to age thirty-three has disappeared—because, although I could have brought out a large number of things while I was stationed in Lisbon, I brought out nothing but a few books. I didn't touch my apartment on strada Palade. I might at least have saved my published books and articles, if not also the manuscripts and notes for works in progress. I can't understand what possessed me to leave everything *there*, although I knew very well what would happen if we lost the war.

15 June

I've given up trying to work on the novel. With some difficulty I compose "Recontre avec Giovanni Papini." I think I could keep right on writing such interviews, with various people: for instance, Jung, Croce, and Ortega.

* * *

I must say somewhere that the prime phenomenon of the twentieth century has not been—and, above all, will not be—the revolution of the proletariat, as the Marxists prophesied seventy or eighty years ago, but the discovery of non-European man and his spiritual universe. I ought to develop this observation in an article. To show that the vision of Marx—the messianism of the proletariat, the final struggle between good and evil, etc.—has its roots and explanation in Judeo-Christian theology, that it is, therefore, integrated into the Mediterranean historical horizon. It would be interesting to discover what exotic and traditional (primitive) civilizations meant for Marx. Now, today, we are beginning to be aware of the nobility and spiritual autonomy of those civilizations. The dialogue with them seems to me more important for the future of European spirituality than is the spiritual revival which the radical emancipation of the proletariat could bring. In the meantime we have seen what "values" the proletariat has revealed to us. Nothing which was not already known to the European spirit.

16 June

I'm writing in bed, in the evening, with some difficulty. I feel I must record at least some of the many, extraordinary particulars I keep learning all the time from Mme. Froebe. Observing my interest in detective novels, she gave me to read *Devil's Guard* by Talbot Mundy (the first English edition appeared under the title *Ransdem*). An occult detective story. With Shambala. Now she's given me another: *There Was a Door*. At night, after I've read for an hour or two "serious things" (Löwith, *Meaning in History;* Jung, *Antwort auf Iob*), I abandon myself to Talbot Mundy. In the morning, at tea, Mme. Froebe asks my impressions. (But I must add that she has "revealed" other books to me also: for instance, those extraordinary *Seven Gothic Tales* by Isak Dinesen, of whom I had never heard, who, she tells me, is a Dutch woman, still alive and residing in South Africa. She has written only a few books, all of them in English.)

Max Pulver, who lectured several times at Eranos, has died. The night after she read the news of his death in a magazine, Mme. Froebe suffered a long attack of insomnia, an unusual thing for her. The following morning she fell into a curiously shaped cement pit, which resembled a coffin. "He's pulling me into the grave after him," she told me. "Exactly as after Van der Leeuw's death. That time I fell on my face, and even before I hit the ground I knew why I had fallen. It was as though someone had caught hold of my heels." Mme. Froebe had then executed a rite of separation from Van der Leeuw, using water. (She didn't describe it to me, but I'll read about it in the place where she read it, the book *Psychic Defence*.) She used the same rite to separate herself from Max Pulver. "I had an aversion to him," she says. "It will be harder."

Mme. Froebe has known a great many people: at first, theosophists, spiritualists, and occultists; then psychologists, philosophers, and orientalists—"professors," as she says with admiration. About Mead, Waite, Robert Eisler, Hauer, Zimmer, and many others she has told me a great many amusing anecdotes, but she is especially indefatigable when she speaks about Jung and "archetypes." For her, Eranos is an archetype. She believes it is situated on the line of Plato's academy. Twenty years of striving, but now Eranos is a "presence," and twenty volumes of *Eranos Jahrbücher* exist in libraries. I can imagine how proud she is of her work. At first, Jung's circle sabotaged her. The

"psychological circle" at Zurich saw Eranos as a competitor. Therefore, they never invited her anywhere. Even Jung behaved very harshly
toward her until a few years ago. She herself, however, recognized a
bond, she felt herself linked to him, "as to Yahweh," she adds, with
whom she now is struggling. Nevertheless, invited with others to
someone's place in Ascona, Jung drank more than usual, forced her to
drink also, and then performed the ritual I mentioned a few days ago.
He removed his ring, which bore the inscription "ABRAXA," and,
placing it in a cup of wine, he recited some mysterious formulas; then
he put it on her finger. The next day when everyone had awakened,
Mme. Froebe said to him: "You, as a psychologist, have done a very
serious thing. You have bound me to you!" Jung replied: "It wasn't I
who did it, but *der Selbst!*"

21 June

        Am reading all sorts of strange books. And every evening I
listen to Mme. Froebe talk about Jung's admirers, about the lecturers'
manias, and about their dreams.
        I'm not the only one, it seems, to have let himself be seduced by
Talbot Mundy's books. Van der Leeuw went up to his room every
evening with a folder of "urgent papers"—and immediately picked up
OM or *There Is a Door.*
        Mme. Froebe before the war invited Berdyayev to Ascona. He accepted,
but he never came. He had no one with whom to leave his dog.

                                        * * *

One of Jung's admirers, a woman of fifty, who lived in a villa in the
mountains several kilometers from Casa Gabriella, learning that Jung bathed
in the lake each morning at 7:00, came a quarter of an hour before and waited
for him on the beach in a bathing suit. (Probably she had gotten up at 5:00.)
She told Jung she liked swimming next to him in Lago Maggiore; she felt
as though she were bathing in the collective unconscious.

25 June

        An enthusiastic letter from Jung after his reading *Le Chaman-
isme.* Of course I give it immediately to Mme. Froebe to read. She

seems very excited. Jung, she assures me, *never* writes about the books of others.

ZURICH, *28 June*

Guests of Dr. Bänziger for two or three days at his villa at Herrliberg, a hamlet twenty minutes from Zürich, on the lakeshore. The house is high up, on a hill. From the garden, looking across several meadows and roofs of houses, your eyes fall directly on the water.

I understand the source of the sudden nostalgia mixed with sweetness that I haven't felt for a long time: the landscape around Lake Zürich resembles (or at least it seems so to me) the hills of Romania.

* * *

Dr. Bänziger listens to me tell about my adventure in a sailboat on the Black Sea: how we were caught in a storm, the mast broke, and we were driven far out into the open waters. Following that adventure experienced at age fifteen or sixteen, I was left with a curious traumatism: I can't stand storms, thunder, and lightning—especially lightning. What makes it so strange, I tell him, is that prior to that time I had really enjoyed thunderstorms. (The year previous I was almost struck by lightning in the Carpathians, because, when the storm broke, I was seized with a Dionysian exhilaration and leapt, screaming, from rock to rock. The lightning struck ten meters from me without, however, diminishing my exhilaration.) During the storm on the sea I kept seeing the huge waves and saying over and over to myself, I'll never come out of this alive! Then I'd shut my eyes. And yet I wasn't left with a phobia for water. I like to swim. I'm happy whenever I can make a journey on the sea.

Dr. Bänziger offers an explanation: when I was in the boat, I didn't realize that I could be struck by lightning. I was afraid of the water only. My fear of the lightning remained in the unconscious; it was not consumed in experience. He believes I ought to try to relive the event someday at home—in order to "realize" that which has remained buried in the unconscious.

BASEL, *1 July*

We arrived here yesterday afternoon at 2:00, in a terrible heat. Immediately we headed for the old city. Beside the cathedral, in the warm, oppressive shade, several men were sleeping on benches. The houses bear their dates above their doors: fourteenth and fifteenth centuries. We Romanians can hardly believe our eyes.

At last, I meet Karl Meuli. We have a long conversation. Sixty years old, but he looks ten or fifteen years younger. He tells me he will never leave the boys' school where he teaches; he prefers this work of secondary-school professor to that of teaching courses in Greek at the university. I confess how much I regret his having lost already seven or eight years of his life preparing a critical edition of the works of Bachofen; in that length of time he could have written a book of his own. He replies that he has no regrets: Bachofen is from Basel. A culture is made by continuous sacrifices for the other's advantage. Moreover, he adds laughing, he is also director of the Swiss Folklore Society. He laughs all the time. A handsome man, gray haired, with a deep, kindly yet penetrating gaze.

This morning, at the Kunstmuseum. Amusing, if not even a bit perfidious—the placing of the Picasso paintings of 1912–22 beside those of Braque from the same period. You look at one, two, or three Braque paintings; then you stop in front of the next picture and discover it is signed by Picasso—ordinarily in the following year. His genius for "stealing the other man's discovery" (as it seems will be recognized some day).

3 July

I left my reading glasses on the train. At the station they tell me the train has gone to Lourdes to be cleaned and won't be back for two or three days. I'm paralyzed. I read with eyes watering, bending my face close to the page. Almost like Papini.

Unbearable heat, as in the summer of 1947.

22 July

Sorel's great historico-political intuitions are due in large measure to psychological divination. The critical analysis which he makes of bourgeois ideology is based almost always on an intuition of a "literary" order, in the sense that he divines the behavior of a certain human type through the same intuitive mechanism with which a novelist understands his characters. For example: what Sorel says in *Illusions du progrès* about the attachment of the bourgeois class to the ideology of infinite progress. The historico-political analysis of this ideological adhesion to a myth is made on a psychological basis. The bourgeoisie, says Sorel, enjoys technological progress and believes that tomorrow the whole world will profit by the results of that progress, in order to be able to enjoy in peace *today* that which it *already* possesses, without any inferiority complex. Because, while it is true that the poor are suffering, technological progress will liberate them too tomorrow. Therefore, we the possessors are justified in enjoying what we have; all the other people will not have long to wait to possess and enjoy it *tomorrow,* as we do today.

ASCONA, *24 August*

I've been here four days, this time alone. Autumn already: rain, fog, cold. The day before yesterday I presented my lecture—with rather good success, I believe. But I made the mistake of speaking about the difficulty Christianity has in assimilating "History," and since then I've had to answer questions continually. Matrons, almost elderly, come and ask me: "How can you not believe that Christianity has brought comfort and hope to suffering humanity?" etc.

* * *

Among the next lecturers, the one I find most interesting is Father D'Arcy. A Jesuit with the face of one damned, he is nervous and sometimes stammers. Extremely thin, with dark, troubled eyes. We get along with each other rather well. He was much pleased with my lecture. Mme. Froebe told me in June how she had come to invite him. At her hairdresser's one day she had seen an "extraordinary photograph" in an illustrated English magazine. "That man must come to Ascona!" she said to herself. She tore the page out of the magazine and took it home. After learning that it was a picture of Father D'Arcy, S.J., she read a book of his and then wrote to invite him. She seemed very gratified that he agreed to come.

Yesterday evening, a lecture by Herbert Read about art. Slides from Picasso and Moore. Strongly influenced by Jung's "archetypes." I had known only his poems and had imagined him rather differently.

* * *

After my lecture, at lunch at Mme. Froebe's, a long conversation with Jung. He agrees to the publication of an interview which *Combat* has asked me to write.

25 August

I return to my room at 6:30 after a long lunch at Casa Gabriella, followed by a two-hour discussion with Jung. Then, at his apartment, seated beside him at the table, taking an interview. I'm exhausted. I start to jot down a few ideas. I shall not, however, be able to speak of the case of the Catholic nun whom he treated for a serious neurasthenic condition, who finally admitted to Jung that she had not believed for many years, not even in God—but who knew now that she would die within the Church. Neither can I speak about Jung's experiences with Freud—about whom he asserted that he had no "psychological insight" and that he had constructed his theory of sexuality out of resentment. In 1907 Jung had a dream, to which I shall make reference in the interview, which he related to Freud. Later Jung saw in it the first allusion to the collective unconscious. Freud told him the meaning was this: that he wished to kill his wife, sister-in-law, and mother-in-law, because in the deep cellar which he had seen in his dream there were a great many bones but only three skulls. On another occasion, at a congress, when Jung was reproaching Freud for mistakenly explaining Akhenaton's reform as a revolt against the father (because all pharaohs eradicated their predecessor's names from inscriptions), Freud fainted.

During our long conversation today I noticed how much he insists on asserting that he too has had "numinous" experiences. He related them to me. Perhaps I'll summarize them in the interview. If not, then here at least.

* * *

In 1912 Jung was engaged in the study of the dissociation of personality. Once, taking the train from Zurich to Schaffhausen (an hour's journey), he remembers only entering a tunnel, and then he comes to his senses hearing the conductor calling out: "Schaffhausen!" He doesn't understand what is wrong with him; he is afraid he's losing his mind, becoming schizophrenic. Because, during that whole time he had been completely dominated by a "waking dream": he saw a map of Europe that was being slowly inundated, country by country, beginning with France and Germany. Soon the whole continent was under water, except for Switzerland; here there seemed to be a high mountain which the waves could not engulf. Jung saw himself standing on that mountain. Looking more closely, he realized that the sea was of blood; on its surface floated corpses, roofs of houses, burned crossbeams, etc.

This waking dream occurred in October 1913. In December it was repeated precisely, again on the occasion of entering the tunnel on the way to Schaffhausen (a penetration into the collective unconscious, he would interpret it later). He becomes more and more preoccupied. A few months later he dreams this dream *three times:* he is with a friend in the South Seas, in the summer—somewhere on the south coast of Sumatra. From the newspapers he learns that a terrible, life-threatening cold wave has struck Europe. Jung decides to go to Batavia to catch a steamship for Europe. His friend, however, says he will travel by sailing vessel from Sumatra to the Hadramat and then go overland through Arabia and Turkey. When Jung reaches Switzerland, snow covers everything. There's an enormous vineyard with great clusters of grapes, frozen. He begins to break off bunches of fruit and give them to the people around him (whom he cannot see).

Since it had been repeated three times, the dream disturbed him greatly. Just then he had to give a paper on schizophrenia for a meeting at Aberdeen. He decided to write about himself. The paper was to be read in midsummer (exactly the period in which, in his dream of the South Seas, he found out that Europe was being ravaged by that mysterious cold wave). He said to himself, probably I'll go mad as soon as the lecture is over. But on 31 July 1914, after he had presented his paper, he learned from the newspapers that war had broken out. He took a ship for Holland. "That morning," he tells me, "there was no one on earth happier than I. I realized that I wasn't crazy and that I wasn't losing my mind. I understood that my dreams had come from the collective unconscious and that their meaning was something entirely different from a presentiment of an attack of schizophrenia."

A little while later he read about the adventurous voyage of the German captain, Von Mucke, in a sailing vessel from Sumatra to the Hadramat. Now, since he had discovered "synchronicity," he interpreted that vision very easily. But it would take me too far afield to comment on it now.

* * *

Freud told him once: "We must impose psychoanalysis as a dogma, in order to defend ourselves from occultism. The West is threatened by occultism."

Jung's comment: he was afraid that phantoms might really *exist*.

Freud's two obsessions: infamy and the Church.

* * *

As they were arriving in New York, Freud looked at the skyscrapers and then turned to Jung: "If they only knew what dynamite we bring with us!"

26 August

A story told by Dr. Riklin: a tram is about to stop at a certain station. Suddenly, without understanding how it happens, the conductor turns the crank and the tram shoots off at top speed. Twenty meters ahead it hits an old man carrying a bundle on a cane over his right shoulder. He is killed on the spot. Dr. Riklin is entrusted with analyzing the conductor. The man remembers nothing, understands nothing. But when he was a boy of fourteen or fifteen, his father was an invalid, paralyzed. A schoolmate, a few years older than he, comes to live with them. Soon his mother becomes pregnant. The boy realizes what has happened. Disgusted, he takes his sister aside and tells her. Just then, the schoolmate comes into the room, carrying a bundle on a stick over his shoulder. Without speaking another word, he leaves and shuts himself in his room. After the accident, the conductor kept having the same dream over and over: he is in the tram, following a man with a bundle over his right shoulder, down various streets. Once, striking the man with the tram and knocking him down, he went to see what was in the bundle: it was a dead baby.

INNSBRUCK, *30 August*

We arrived this evening, and after refusing several offers of "private rooms" made right on the station platform (two women smiled at us and begged: "The hotel is too expensive! Our room is clean and it costs only fifteen shillings!), we decide on an ordinary hotel, rather far away, on Maximillianstrasse. It is called the Speckbucher. We leave immediately for the old city. I was here a quarter of a century ago. I remember only the Inn River, whose purple waters flow fast, and the old quarter around the tower.

Both last night and again this morning, when we return to the narrow streets, I have the same vague feeling of bliss. In my memories, "the Germanic" is connected with youth and melancholy. Impossible for me to understand why, but sometimes I feel that during the first half of the nineteenth century I lived in a German town. Several times I had a rather strange "waking dream": I saw an old man dressed in a long overcoat that came down to his knees. He wore a strange kind of cap with a bill. He appeared to be an engineer (*later* I knew he was connected with the railroad). Sometimes this disturbing detail: although he lived in a German city, he wasn't German but from the Baltic region. He spoke Russian well. I "saw" him once (*later*) standing in the snow beside a primitive locomotive. All the time I had the feeling that that man *was I*. Yet absolutely nothing connected us; I recognized nothing of my inner being in him. He was a railroad engineer. Nothing "spiritual" in his bearded face, hidden under a cap, dreaming of nothing but engines and locomotives. And yet, I felt that *I was like that* or, more precisely, that *I was he*. With no other human image from my frequent daydreams have I sensed such a close identity.

That man lived in Germany. He loved that land.

ALPBACH, *1 September*

Since the evening of the day before yesterday, here at Europäische College where I was so imprudent as to agree, last spring (when the end of August seemed so far away!), to direct a seminar on the history of religions. Since yesterday, a steady rain. Only now, in the evening, does the weather seem ready to improve.

At Hotel Böglerhof along with the other lecturers. I meet again with Kerényi and Löwith, and for the first time I meet Professor Antoni from Rome, who tells me many sensational things about Vittorio Macchioro, one of my adolescent "passions."

Alexander Auer, the multilingual secretary of the college, makes an excellent impression on me: the old Austria—cosmopolitan, a little skeptical, mad about music.

Even in the rain we take long walks. The elevation here is a thousand meters. Tyrolian landscape—but I'm constantly reminded of the Carpathians, the Bucegis, of summer vacations. I haven't climbed a Romanian mountain since the summer of 1939. Here I recover the ruggedness, the rain, the air of those other peaks.

6 September

There have been just two clear days. The rest of the time, a cold, heavy, fine autumnal rain. The atmosphere of a mountain chalet.

For the past four mornings, from 9:00 until 12:00, I have conducted the seminar on the history of religions. We met in different places: around tables, in the courtyard, on the terrace, in the room. An interesting group. Polemical dialogue with Kerényi.

We leave tomorrow for Kupfstein, on the German frontier. Ghiţă Racoveanu is coming to take us in Father Popan's car.

MUNICH, 10 September

I no longer recognize the city. Impossible to remember that I was here in 1936 or 1937. The whole downtown area was destroyed. The new buildings which have been built make it resemble a sector of any other "modern" European city. We drive to Garmisch, Linderhof, and Oberammergau.

13 September

Enroute to Bonn, in Father Popan's car. This evening, at Rudesheim, we enter Der Drosselhof Bierhaus on the famous street of barrels. "Rhenish" atmosphere. I recall the years 1935–37, the Rhine valley. As usual, I return to the past, make plans, promise myself to reread authors I haven't touched in ten or fifteen years.

The "concentrated time" of travel. Like that of the dramatic performance. (I promise myself to take up again the "theory" of concentrated time, sketched in *Noaptea de Sânziene,* in a philosophic essay.)

* * *

At Bonn, Dorotheenstrasse 141: Spaltmann's home. We meet his wife, a legendary figure about whom we have heard so much. In the final weeks of the war, Spaltmann, despite his heart condition, was drafted into a unit of shock troops—which did not exist, however, except on paper. His wife came every morning with both a thermos of hot water for shaving and another thermos with coffee—and, in spite of age-old Germanic discipline, she went all the way to his quarters on the grounds reserved exclusively for military personnel. Spaltmann relates Shakespearean scenes: a few days before the collapse of Germany, an SS general gave a pathetic, demented speech, urging them to fall to the last man, in defense of the Reich. In the background—the noise of cannons and Allied planes flying very low, strafing. Beside the SS general, standing calmly with her dinner pail and full thermoses, was Frau Spaltmann, our girl from Braşov. She listened to him, and when he had finished his speech, she calmly walked over to Spaltmann and handed him the thermos of coffee. The spectacle was so implausible that no one dared to intervene.

PARIS, *26 September*

As usual, I return to Hegel. This has been happening for the past five or six years, since I've been wrestling with the meaning of "history." I return to Hegel two or three times a year. I read for hours, for days in a row, from whatever books of his I have available—but especially from the texts translated and annotated by Kojéve and Hyppolite.

I observe that Hegel's decision (on 14 September 1800) to reconcile himself with his time, to transcend the scission between the "absolute finitude'' of interior existence and the "absolute infinitude'' of the objectivity of the exterior world—I observe that this "virile unification with time (= history)'' closely resembles the decision of my generation to "adhere'' to politics in order to integrate itself into the historical moment and to defend itself from the "abstract,'' to avoid retreat into unreality. The same explanation seems to me valid for understanding the adherence of intellectuals to communism. The interpretation Hegel gives to the destiny of Hölderlin and to the Romantics in general—that "not to live in your own house in the world is more than a personal misfortune; it is a 'nontruth' '' and that "the most terrible destiny consists in not having a destiny''—reminds me of the polemics of the "historicists'' against the intellectuals who did not "adhere'' during 1935–38. I find the same positions restated in the polemics of the French Communists and Existentialists, and they are, probably, attested everywhere.

Here I see the great temptation of the Spirit, which very few resist. The grave threat that you will be deprived of your destiny, that you will be thrown into the "dustbin of history,'' etc., is a kind of blackmail which almost invariably ends in getting the better of you. You "adhere'' in order to save yourself, in order to remain in "life,'' in "history.'' And then, for the same reason, you sign declarations that say exactly the opposite of what you believe, you make self-criticisms, you accept the condemnation of the people's tribunal which interprets the "Spirit of the Time.'' I must analyze someday this grave error, validated and transfigured by Hegel, which drives intellectuals to renounce their proper vocation. Show the limits within which the "historical moment'' can be accepted.

And since I'm still on the "Hegel chapter,'' let me note an observation I made a long while ago, when I first became acquainted with the writings of Hegel's youth (in Jean Hyppolite's studies). I was "pleasantly surprised'' then to discover that, until his Jena period, Hegel did not attack philosophical problems head on—or, more precisely, he did not meditate on texts and problems of philosophy—but investigated religion and history directly, from their sources; his principal preoccupation was the *historically concrete,* the life of peoples, the "spirit" that manifests itself directly in that life. In these long years of historical researches, Hegel prepared his later philosophical vision. He hammered out the concepts of *Phänomenologie* not by meditating or speculating "in the abstract" but by struggling to understand the *Volksgeist*.

Now, this makes me happy, because it validates my own philosophical "method." I've devoted almost thirty years of my life to "concrete" studies: philology, history, folklore, religions. Always, however, I have had as my final objective the understanding of the spiritual meaning of the materials I was studying. This is what C. Noica came to see eventually, when (after begging me for years to return to philosophy and give up erudition!) he wrote me that he understood the meaning and fruitfulness of my works of specialization.

5 October

Dr. Hunwald loans me a copy of *The Great Beast: The Life of Aleister Crowley* by John Symonds, and I read it in two days. Not since *The Search for Corvo,* which I read hastily during the winter of 1940–41 at Oxford, have I run across such a captivating biography. I had heard of Crowley long ago, but I knew almost nothing about him. All I knew was that he was a "Satanist" and that he was involved in black magic and tantrism. Symonds's biography reveals a bizarre individual, half madman and half humbug, but not devoid of grandeur. I am especially impressed by his struggle to break himself of his addiction to opium, cocaine, and heroin. Amazing sexual and vital capacities. He ingested eight times more heroin than the amount sufficient to kill a man. His "magical rituals" were, in reality, sexual rites. Undoubtedly, he applied some of the techniques of tantrism, but I don't know how he discovered them. On one page of his journal he records that "the magical rite" lasted six hours. Such a thing could not be done except by means of a precise, tantric technique—but how did he manage to learn it, since he accepted no discipline and could not claim any Indian "initiation"?

Am amused to discover that he too was in Lisbon, Estoril, and Cascaes, that he had there an adventure and tried to deceive everybody, making it seem he had committed suicide by throwing himself into the Boca do Inferno—when, in reality, he had left Portugal and had rejoined his lady friend in Berlin. He had been invited to Portugal by that strange poet, Fernando Pessoa, whom I once liked very much.

All I read from his private diaries fascinated me. Robust, vigorous, concentrated prose. Even when he records cruelties, profanities, and demented acts, his language does not lose its density or precision. I admire especially the lucidity with which he notes both the symptoms of intoxication and his frequent failures in his battle with the temptation of heroin. He records the hour—sometimes even the minute—when he was drained of all strength or overcome by melancholy.

4 November

A few days ago I read in a newspaper that someone had written the Centre d'informations, recently established in Paris, asking for a photograph of Attila. I don't know whether the story is true. But I found myself suddenly reacting against the joke the author of the article made of it. Why does ignorance of historical events seem such a grave thing to us? It's a sign, a symptom, of our era; no longer dare we ignore history, because we claim to be constituted exclusively by it, by History. That is why all our education, academic and nonacademic, gives greater and greater weight to History and chronology.

This made me think about other cultures—that of India, for example (I speak, of course, of traditional India). Almost no Indian can name the century—and not even approximately the "era"—of the great historical personalities. This indifference to chronology is general, and it has a profound philosophical meaning. Education takes place on two planes, the only planes considered theoretically valid for India: metaphysics (and, therefore, liberation) and tradition. The youth learns the essential things. If he follows a course of instruction oriented toward metaphysics, he learns about Being and Nonbeing, illusion and freedom, etc. If he remains in the world, education teaches him tradition, which has no love for chronology or history. The young man or woman learns how to act, how to greet people, how to eat, talk, pray, etc. An Indian girl knows more abut men, sexuality, and marriage than does her occidental counterpart, even if the latter was kissed at age ten and has known physical love since fourteen or fifteen. Traditional Indian education reveals the *meaning* of these countless gestures and behaviors which constitute public and private life. In what respect is the woman who learned in school about Attila and knows in what century he lived superior to the young Indian woman who is quite ignorant of chronology but knows how to *behave* toward family members and strangers; who knows the meaning of love and sexuality; who knows how to look at the sky, the water, and the earth; who knows how to pick a flower, what to say to the trees, and many other such things? Which of them learns more—and more that is essential—about *being* and about *mankind?*

27 November

Back at 62½ rue de la Tour for the past few days. Dr. Laforgue has lent us his apartment until April. Too bad it's so dark here. On the vacant lot across the street, where sometimes at night we used to see a little light, like the window of a cottage (I never knew whether there was a cottage there or only the lantern of a vagrant hiding among the weeds behind the board fence), a seven-story apartment block is being erected now. It's almost finished. The same thing at the corner, on avenue Paul Doumer: nine floors. We have to have the lamps lit from 2:00 P.M., and sometimes, when it's overcast, even from the time we get up in the morning.

A day before leaving rue Duhesme, I dispatched to Roger Caillois the article, "La Nostalgie du paradis," for *Diogène*. It was the last important scientific work I had left to do.

Here, I have returned to literature. I'm almost finished with a short story, a fantasy, "12.000 capete de vită" (Twelve Thousand Head of Cattle). I've had it in mind for five years. Once on rue Vaneau I started to write it, but there was too much noise in the room next door, and I gave up the effort.

14 December

I'm writing with black ink now in order not to tire my eyes too much. In the light of the lamp, the "South-Seas blue" ink was almost invisible, as if I'd written in some colorless fluid.

* * *

After finishing "12.000 capete de vită," I read the novel again. I was in despair. The beginning seemed extremely weak. Last year, at Monte Carlo, although I felt that the first two chapters were not yet perfected, I gave them to Christinel to type, just to be able to go on, to finish the first part. I ought to have made an effort then to "validate" the beginning, to augment the substances of Ioana, Ileana, and Ştefan. The main characters of this novel are the least successful ones. (And this owing to my unfortunate idea of "saving" the Vădastra novel, written ten years ago at Lisbon, by integrating it into the new novel whose characters had not yet been articulated.)

Finally, I took up the work again, creeping on hands and knees. I abandoned the "prologue." The book will open with Vădastra. I reworked all the passages in which Ioana and Ştefan appear. I believe Ioana is beginning to take form. But I'm still not finished with revisions. I won't be able to begin part 2 before next week. Thus, I shall have lost, altogether, three weeks. And I can't even work on it all the time. I'm also writing bread-and-butter texts.

24 December

Christmas Eve. Fine rain. The cold wave of the past week has abated. A February air. But it's so dark that for the past two days I've worked by lamplight even in the mornings.

On Sunday, 21 December, I began the first chapter of part 2. I'm on page 12. I promise myself that this time I'll *work* on the novel, that is, correct and transcribe each chapter several times, until I'm satisfied.

25 December

We dine alone, Christinel and I. In the morning I began writing on the novel, and I continued all afternoon. Extraordinarily sad—but I forget my sadness while I'm working. The sadness that comes over me whenever I return to *Noaptea de Sânziene*.

31 December

I've been working every day, but there are few pages. Am up to page 30. And yet, since I resumed work on the novel, I've done nothing else.

Undated, 1952
    Notes for a postscript to *Le Chamanisme.*
    1. Stress the importance of shamanism for a comparative history of mysticism. The ecstatic experience of the shaman represents the mystical experience specific to archaic religions. The inadequacy (in fact, the error) of a universal history of mysticism that would begin, for instance, with the *Rig Veda* or the *Tao-te-Ching,* would present Orphism, Gnosticism, Yoga, Buddhism, tantrism and would develop in detail the morphology of mysticism in the three monotheisms—but would pass over in silence the ecstatic experiences of the shaman. Now, what characterizes this type of ecstatic experience is the shaman's celestial ascent, his meeting with the god, and the conversation that takes place—in other words, his recovery (it's true, only provisionally and only *in spirit*) of the situation of primordial man, the mythical ancestor, who, in the beginning, *in illo tempore,* was capable of reaching Heaven and conversing directly with the divinity. In a sense, shamanic ecstasy is a recovery of the original paradisiacal situation which existed before the "fall."
    2. Now, this ecstatic experience has its correspondence to a certain Christian mystical tradition, namely, that *raptus mysticus* to which St. Paul alludes in 2 Corinthians, in which he was "caught up into Paradise and heard unspeakable words which it is not permitted for a man to utter" (12.4). From this point of view, archaic mysticism (i.e., shamanism) is situated closer to the Pauline experience (which founds the *first* Christian mystical tradition) than are other mysticisms, more complex and infinitely more prestigious, elaborated in India and the Far East.
    3. The role of the shaman appears even more decisive in what we could term the *experiental knowledge of death.* The shaman learns to know death in the course of his initiation, when he goes for the first time into the underworld and is tortured by spirits and demons. After initiation, he knows how to descend into Hell, in order to search for the soul of the sick man (stolen away by demons) or to guide the souls of the dead to their new abode—and he succeeds in reaching there and

returning to earth because he *knows the way.* The ecstatic experiences of the shaman have contributed in large measure to the establishment and articulation of a mythical geography of death, together with a mythology specific to death. The central motif of this funereal geography and this mythology of death is found also in the epic poetry of many peoples (of Central Asia, Polynesia, etc.) and in universal folklore. But the importance of ecstatic experiences in the spiritual history of archaic humanity is not limited to the artistic creations they have caused. To *see* and to *describe* the conditions of postmortem existence reduces the terror of death. Moreover, the *heroism* of the shaman who confronts death for the good of others strengthens and fortifies the faith of man in his own mode of being. The shaman becomes a *model,* because he shows that *something can be done,* that demons can be conquered and that illnesses provoked by them can be cured; because he demonstrates that death itself can be "understood" and therefore controlled.

Thus, the unknown and terrifying world of death *takes form,* acquires a structure and even a geography. The infernal personages become *visible;* death is equated with a rite of passage into a new mode of being, a "spiritual" one; that is, it ends by constituting an *initiation.*

1 January 1953

New Year's Eve party at Dr. and Mme. Dolto-Marette's place. We return home at 2:00 with Père Bruno, our neighbor.

Today, at 7:00 P.M., I finish chapter 1. Then I go out for a walk. Rain. Tonight, snow. At 10:00, while I was passing in front of the Trocadero, the snow that covered the trees and grounds, making them white, reminded me suddenly of winters in the homeland.

I continue to feel sad, but I know it can't be helped. The destiny of *Noaptea de Sânziene.*

4 January

I write every day, and at night I transcribe. Am at page 8 of chapter 2. But sometimes I feel so sad, so discouraged, that I wonder whether it may not be a sign of something else. The episodes I'm working on are rather sad ones, but is that all it is? I keep thinking of home and my family. No news from them in a long time. I'm afraid of what might have happened. Everything was left there: my youth, my past, family, friends. All I did and didn't do, papers from adolescence, correspondence from so many friends no longer living, books, file folders with my first articles from lycée and university days—absolutely everything. Here, in the "West," I am only a fragment.

13 January

For several days I've been working badly, reluctantly. A slight cold last week and a new series of small annoyances have been enough to dissipate my "lust for literature." Whole days spent in writing one page. Have transcribed chapter 1. Am well along in chapter 2, but I wonder whether I've succeeded in giving it the intensity it merits. Sometimes I'm tempted to set it aside and to begin again on the second edition of *Yoga,* for which Payot is waiting. But I stubbornly persist. It's my bad luck that whenever a "lust for literature" takes hold of me, I'm shackled to scientific works—and then, when I become free again, my "lust" quickly leaves me. Does this indicate an estrangement from literature? The drying up of my epic springs? An incapacity for creation?

25 January

This evening I finished chapter 2. Rather long, almost 60 pages. Since I worked hard all the time, without "inspiration," I transcribed it as I went along, so that today I have a finished manuscript. Tomorrow, Monday, God willing, I'll start chapter 3. But on the twenty-eighth the Godels will arrive from Egypt, and again I'll spend a week in philosophical and scientific discussions, distancing myself from literature.

28 January

The Godels have arrived. I call a halt to the novel until the evening of 5 February. Anyhow, this pause comes at a good time. My "inspiration" can barely move. I still don't understand what's wrong with me. I tire very quickly. After a few weeks, any book I'm writing begins to bore me. Another detail that exasperates me: when I recover freedom for literature, I no longer have the urge to write. I've done everything I could to cheer myself up in these past three or four months. Other than an average of ten or twelve letters a week, I have no obligations. I stay at my desk for seven or eight hours, but I work effectively for only three or four. For the rest, I transcribe, daydream, or read. Maybe my health is also to blame. I work continually by lamplight; I go out very seldom; a beginning of ''vagotonia.''

7 February

In the past two days, I've worked rather well. The light outdoors has allowed me to write without a lamp until 3:00 P.M. Progress, however, is still rather slow. It's as though I don't dare to approach the deaths of those many characters I've been carrying around inside me for several years. Chapter 3 brings the death of Cătălina. I'd become very fond of that girl. When I first imagined her in the summer of 1949, she had a colorless role and she was insufferable. But in time I discovered a wonderful soul. It's a pity she was so unlucky. I'm sorry I chose for her the life and especially the death she will have in the novel. I could write another book with nothing but her melancholies and reveries.

8 February

Yesterday I received a copy of Paule Régnier's *Journal.* I had read several enthusiastic articles about this unstable writer, who loved Paul Drouot so much and who committed suicide two years ago out of despair and poverty. I leaf through the *Journal.* Very compact, written to be published. Probably Paule Régnier will regain contemporaneity and may, perhaps, survive through this journal rather than through her books. And that disturbs me. I reflect anew on the purpose of a writer's journal. Gide, Jünger, and others wrote them in order to have them published one day. Hence, they are, as it were, books with ''messages,'' even if they are more direct and episodic. A great many things that can be said only in a journal.

But then, what will I do with all these pages I carry around with me? I ought to forbid from now on that they be published in their entirety. I write in order to be able to reread later. I don't care whether someone else reads me later, but I don't write for him. I write to find myself again later, to remind myself of times uselessly lost (*all* "times" are irreparably condemned, however much we may endeavor to save them).

But perhaps someday I ought to begin to check myself, to write with more care. To *say something*. Such an effort would be advantageous to me—to me above all.

13 February

Finished chapter 3 today.

19 February

A few weeks ago Guillermou brought me the French translation of chapter 2, part 1. Only today do I muster the courage to read it carefully in order to annotate it before passing it on to Christinel to type. Discouragement soon takes hold of me. I have the impression that *Noaptea de Sânziene* loses 100 percent in translation. More precisely, the translation illumines all too harshly the naïvetés and imperfections of the book.

25 February

At Virgil and Monica's new residence, on rue Cassini. It is located in a neighborhood I find delightful, close to the observatory, with many trees and wide, empty streets. We listen to records: "Das Lied von der Erde" by Mahler, Schumann's concerto for piano and orchestra, and some Negro spirituals.

I borrow from them a copy of *The Idiot*. For several days, a strong desire to read it again. The last time I read it was in May 1938 when I was staying at Vrabie's house. This evening I begin it—and I reflect on my own novel. What an unfortunate inspiration I had to spread the action over twelve years! I created for myself a great number of insoluble problems—above all, that of the passage of time. I'd like to finish it right now, so I could start another novel with the plot limited in time to a few days or weeks. Only that way could I give it the density that I feel any truly "epic" action merits.

26 February

Yesterday, together with Guillermou, I corrected the translated chapter, and we were amused to find Romanian terms which, when translated literally into French, exaggerate considerably the meaning of the original text. Ştefan, after he has spoken for some time, "se opreşte deodată, istovit" (stops suddenly, tired). By translating *istovit* by *épuisé* (exhausted), the character seems neuropathic or really ill. This makes me think that the grandiose impression which Russian literature makes on us when read in translation is due in large measure to discrepancies between the original meaning of the adjectives and the equivalents to which the translators have resorted. In the original, characters in Russian novels are much less demented, demonical, and unpredictable than they are in translation.

4 March

I'd forgotten this detail from *The Idiot:* that Muishkin understands the importance of time for historical man, "fallen man." Here is what he says: "A cet moment . . . j'ai entrevu le sens de cette singulière expression: 'il n'y aura plus de temps' (Apocalypse X.6)" [At that moment I glimpsed the meaning of that strange expression: "time shall be no more" (Revelation 10:6)]. The "moment" was the last flash of consciousness before the attack of epilepsy. It is interesting that Dostoevsky understood the *metaphysical* (and not only the *ecstatic*) value of that atemporal "instant," that *nunc stans* which signifies eternity.

22 March

A week ago, seeing that I was wasting my time for nothing and that the novel was scarcely progressing at all, I interrupted it and returned to *Yoga*. Working day and night since then, I've finished in a week chapter 5, the only one for which materials were assembled long ago and for which the bibliography was completed.

24 March

Yesterday and today I wrote, for *Caiete de dor,* a text of thirty-nine pages: "Fragment autobiografic." I had promised it a year ago to Virgil Ierunca. The subject ("How do I reconcile science with literature?") excited me, but I never found time to write about it. Yesterday morning I went to work on it, and by evening I had written twenty-four pages—as in the good old days. Today I finished it. I am satisfied.

27 March

For the past several days I've been reworking that unfortunate chapter 4 of the novel, and I hope to be able to finish it soon. I worked on it for weeks. It was going badly and very slowly. Then, disgusted, I abandoned it and returned to *Yoga*. But writing the article for *Caiete de dor* was enough to cause the "literary passion" to tempt me again. On the other hand, Spaltmann keeps insisting that I not stop work on the novel but finish it as soon as possible.

6 April

This morning I concluded chapter 4. Three chapters remain to be written to finish the novel. I don't know when I'll write them. In two weeks I'll be at Zurich, and until then I must prepare my course for the Jung-Institut and write a number of articles and reviews. Only at Ascona, at the end of May, will I be free again, for four weeks.

7 April

A young Italian philosopher, Abrami, who comes to see me with an introduction from Papini, brings me sad news. In November, Papini suffered a paralyzing stroke. He can no longer walk, and he can write only with great difficulty. His mind remains lucid, but he has aged terribly. It seems probable that *Giudizio universale* will remain unfinished.

11 April

Letters, letters! The day before yesterday I wrote five, yesterday nine, and today I'm on the sixth already—and I still have a whole pile left to answer. It is a mania of mine which has cost me dearly: I like to receive "correspondence." Unfortunately, I receive numerous uninteresting letters from strangers who ask me for interviews on questions of ethnology, psychology, etc., and I defend myself as best I can—especially by lying! In order to refuse proposals for lectures, articles, or interviews on scientific subjects, I lie constantly, saying that I'm ill or that I've left Paris or am on the verge of leaving, etc. I record this detail in order to nullify almost 90 percent of my correspondence: I do not acknowledge it. What I write there very seldom corresponds to reality. I must lie in order to defend my freedom. I admire those who write a letter with the same care with which they redact books. But I don't have time for that sort of thing. Even my books betray me sometimes, because I never wait a few months before sending them to the publisher—in order to view them "from a distance." Only after they appear do I become aware of their imperfections.

Why do I do all this? Because I feel that I have a great many more things to say before being able to say the *essential*. So I prefer to publish imperfect books, thus ridding myself of a load of observations, materials, and "ideas" that are crushing me, in the hope that in the near future I shall again become free to write my books—rather than to wait for the maturation of those "ideas," etc. and draft my books with greater care (i.e., above all, to hold them in a drawer for a few months after they've been written); had I done this, I'd still be working today on *Traité and Le Mythe,* and I wouldn't even have started on *Le Chamanisme.* Thus I would still be some twenty to twenty-five years' distance from my *essential* books.

MEILEN, *22 April*

I arrived the day before yesterday (alone; Christinel went with Anne Hunwald to Italy). The guest of Dr. Franz Rilkin at his villa at Meilen, about thirty kilometers from Zürich. The house is on a hill overlooking the lake; and immediately behind the house the forest begins. I have a little attic room. I hear a spring in the forest, and I hear those hundreds of birds whose chirping I had forgotten since leaving Casa Gabriella. There is a divine, unbelievable peacefulness here. Since three days ago, spring has come, abundant and warm. I crossed a Switzerland whose trees were all in bloom. At last I've escaped from the cold, darkness, and dampness of the past two weeks on rue de la Tour! Here I've changed my schedule. I go to bed at 11:00 and wake up before 7:00. I hope to be able to work well, either on *Yoga* or on the novel.

Last night I presented my first lecture, two hours in length, at the Jung-Institut. About twenty persons present, but mostly medical doctors, professors, priests. (And one priest is a German Orthodox.) I spoke without using a text. People seemed interested. Mme. Jung also came to the lecture. She tells me that the professor has been rather ill all winter. Tracheitis. He was hardly able to work. His strength allowed him only to put together a series of old articles for a new volume.

23 April

At Herrliberg, to see Bänziger, I stay for lunch. I find him tired and weak. He has read *Images et symboles,* and, although he seems enthusiastic, he says that I have minimized Freud's work. I reply that, not being a psychologist, I am unable to judge either the technique or the theory of Freud. But I have a right to say that his explanations of religious experiences and other spiritual activities are purely and simply inept. Bänziger agrees. Freud, he says, was a materialist and a positivist of the lowest order.

1 May

Superb day. I had begun chapter 5 in a fine frame of mind, almost "inspired," when I received a telegram from Georgel Deme-trescu in Madrid, asking me to send him urgently, by air mail, the text of the lecture I was requested to give in connection with "Romanian Week." I proposed this solution to him a week ago, but since I had received no word from him, I had supposed they had rejected the proposal and had called on someone else. Now I have to write twenty-five pages in three days.

5 May

I've written about twelve pages of chapter 5. Not a definitive version, because I skipped over descriptions, merely sketched the junctures between the scenes, etc., contenting myself with writing only the essential. Rather well satisfied. This chapter will have a boisterous tempo.

6 May

Today I wrote eight pages. If only I could have a whole week free, without the course at the institute, without meetings with Jungians, without lectures . . . !

8 May

Invited to take lunch at Jung's house, on Seestrasse, in Küsnacht. A house crammed full of things: paintings, furniture, art objects, books. I regret, however, that I didn't see the library: those hundreds of volumes on alchemy about which Corbin has told me. I find Jung unchanged, although he was ill all winter. One detail: he walks with a cane now. It is not the cane of an invalid, however, but the crosier of a bishop, the staff of a patriarch. His eyes are still as much alive as ever, his voice strong, his laugh deep and full. He still eats with the same appetite I knew at Ascona, and he talks just as much. He tells me many amusing anecdotes and details. His discussions with philosophers in India—about the unconscious. Dasgupta's visit here at Küsnacht in 1939 when he stayed for a week: in the evening he recited some of his own poems, translating them into English.

Jung tells me about something that happened to Robert Eisler when he was a young man. He had come to Vienna to examine a codex at the Ambrosiana, and he stole it! All the frontier posts were alerted, and he was arrested on the train, with the codex in his pocket. Before the commissioner of police he declared that while he was at the library he had received a telegram from his mistress in Vienna informing him that she was leaving him. Eisler said he had been so shocked that he put the codex in his pocket and left immediately for the station without even going to his hotel first. This theft and arrest provoked a scandal—"*even* in Vienna," Jung adds in conclusion.

He told me also that Eisler—who knew all and read all—had an original theory about finances and, in particular, about the protection and increase of wealth. He even tried to make Jung rich by revealing to him secrets for multiplying capital.

* * *

This evening I receive an enthusiastic letter from Monica Ierunca about *Nuntă în Cer*. Terrible melancholy, remembering how I wrote that book.

Also an article by Jacques Masui in *Les Cahiers du Sud:* "Mythes et symboles selon Mircea Eliade." This is the first study about my philosophical work to appear in French, and I ought to be proud. But I keep thinking about *Nuntă în Cer* and *Noaptea de Sânziene* (on which I worked not at all today, because the discussions with Jung have drawn me out of the world of literature again). It seems to be the case, with my literary activity, that, whenever I begin writing the novel with gusto, visits and obligations intrude and prevent me from continuing.

10 May

This morning I awakened to find snow falling. In half an hour, everything was white, as in the dead of winter. A thick, compact snow.

Now it has stopped falling and is beginning to melt slowly. I hear the birds in the woods again, chirping in confusion, as though a catastrophe had occurred.

I have ahead of me a good afternoon to write, all to myself. Here in this attic chamber, I find again my little attic on strada Melodiei.

11 May

A marvelous day, clear, cold.

Yesterday, as well as the day before, I wrote very well. Am on page 42, almost two-thirds through the chapter. But I don't yet dare to reread it. I want to finish the chapter first, then begin the corrections and copying. I'm trying out this new "system"—of pressing ahead without looking back, realizing I'll have to rewrite certain passages in their entirety.

12 May

Yesterday evening I went again to Dr. Schoppe's to meet Professor Boss and two other psychiatrists. Boss keeps asking me questions about yoga and Indian philosophy, and I seem to be talking almost all the time. Boss is a friend of Heidegger; he sees him every other two or three months; he took him once all the way to Italy in his car. He tells me about the immense number of Heidegger's manuscripts. But most interesting to me is what he said about the resemblance between the present thought of Heidegger and Indian philosophy (the Upanishads, Vedanta—i.e., the texts Boss knows). He assures me that Heidegger has read nothing of Indian philosophy. But the symmetry is explained, perhaps, by the effort he makes to retrace philosophical thought from the pre-Socratics on.

   All this makes me reflect, as I return home on the train, about the "timeliness" of my researches in the history of religions and folklore. What a sure instinct I've had, addressing myself since student days to "exotic" and "popular" spiritual universes and turning away from the study of Western philosophy. "Instinct," in a manner of speaking. It was this that interested me, that "enthused" me. In the autobiographical text I wrote for *Caiete de dor* I do not speak about these things; I don't insist on the correspondence between my theoretical preoccupations and the movement of European philosophy, a movement striving to recover the forms of atemporal knowledge. But someday I ought to show how many secret threads link my theoretical work to the current crisis in occidental thought. The importance I accord to Time, for instance. Significant in this regard is the interest which my texts about Time and History have provoked among psychologists and psychiatrists.

* * *

Speaking with Dr. Schoppe about Freud and remarking that Freudian "explanations" of religion and art seem to me both infantile and demented, he cites the definition of man given by an English psychoanalyst: "We are born mad; then we acquire morality and become stupid and unhappy; then we die." Cioran will like that one!

18 May

   The fifth and final lecture at the institute. I speak freely, "inspired," with an exceptional verve, and I say things which to me seem very interesting. I am unable to judge, however, to what extent I am understood by my audience—who, for the most part, are enchanted by Jung's psychology and are incapable of tasting an idea if they don't know how to valorize it by integrating it into the dimensions of the collective unconscious and the archetypes.

ASCONA, *20 May*

We arrive this evening at Casa Gabriella. A torrid sky, covered with thick clouds; a thunderstorm in the making. This time we aren't staying in the large room with the terrace which we had last year but in the room where the phantom monk appeared earlier (see my journal for last year). As usual, Mme. Froebe has placed on my worktable a number of mediocre books. And the stack will grow each day, because Mme. Froebe has the habit of giving me more books all the time. In this intense "atmosphere," with discussions about alchemy and Gnosis, amid the files of the Eranos Archives—I must write my novel.

23 May

. . . And in spite of all these things, I have been writing very well! I believe that with luck I can finish chapter 5, which was begun on the morning of 1 May, before Thursday, when I must prepare my lecture for the Psychology Club in Zürich.

Spaltmann writes me that he is very pleased with chapter 4. He finds it the most successful one in part 2.

26 May

I finished chapter 5 today, and I hope to finish transcribing it tonight. It is rather lengthy, some sixty pages. Devoted almost wholly to Bibicescu. All the secondary characters—"secondary" at the moment I first visualized them—attain an unexpected dignity on the threshold of their death. Ştefan remains only a witness to the events of their lives and their deaths; sometimes Ştefan seems to be merely a "connecting agent" between the diverse groups of characters, a subject who is passive toward the events which, for others, become their destinies. But I wonder whether the reader will be aware of this role of *witness* which Ştefan plays—witness in the sense of Dante descending into Hell, passing through Purgatory, ascending into Heaven, and listening, recording, and understanding messages. It is very probable that the reader will be disappointed—as, in a sense, I am also—with the colorless role that the principal character, Ştefan, plays. But this destiny of *witness* and "connecting agent" Ştefan has acquired by himself, quite against my own wishes as author.

30 May

Yesterday I was in Zurich to present a lecture: "The Conjunction of Shiva and Shakti in Tantrism," at the Psychology Club. About forty persons, happily several medical doctors, psychologists, and professors among them. I spoke almost two hours. Only afterward did I realize I had spoken in too "erudite" a manner for an audience made up principally of women of a certain age, accustomed to generalities and twaddle about "symbolism."

1 June

I begin chapter 6. Two pages written, with which I'm only half satisfied. How "inspired" I was last week! But all that zest for literature was, actually, the consequence of my annoyance at having to go to Zurich to give a lecture at the Psychology Club. That's how it usually happens with me: I don't like to do—that is, to *write*—what I'm *forced* to do. When I consecrate myself to a book, determined to finish it at all costs, I'm seized soon afterward with a desire to write *something else!*

2 June

After a period of serious illness about five or six years ago, Jung told Mme. Froebe: "It seemed as though I were in a valley full of diamonds, and I was allowed to fill my pockets with diamonds and to take as many in my hands as I could carry—but no more than that. I have a few years left to live, and I'd like to tell as much as I can of what I understood then, when I was ill, but I realize I won't succeed in expressing more than an infinitesimal part, that I'll not be able to show more than one or two diamonds, although my pockets are full of them."

9 June

Chapter 6 goes forward with difficulty–not only because of my faltering "inspiration" but also owing to letters and news I'm receiving. Today comes an invitation to give a lecture at the Rencontres internationales de Genève in September. François Mauriac and Robert Schumann will be attending from France. I tell myself that Romania must be represented—although I know that my own work will be paralyzed for many weeks again.

10 June

An extraordinary letter from Étienne Gilson, with such lavish words of appreciation that I hardly dare reproduce them: "Je ne doute pas que vous ne soyez cité quelque jour par les historiens de la philosophie comme ayant ouvert des perspectives, ignorées jusqu'á vous, sur la préhistoire de la métaphysique du temps chez Platon, Plotin et saint Augustin" [I have no doubt that you will be cited someday by historians of philosophy as having opened perspectives, heretofore ignored, on the prehistory of the metaphysics of time in the thought of Plato, Plotinus, and St. Augustine]. Etc., etc. I am very sincerely *moved*. I remember suddenly that autumn day in 1925 when I began to read Gilson's little book on medieval philosophy (published by Payot), and I caught myself saying out loud: "This is thrilling, thrilling!" I was in my attic room on strada Melodiei. I was so hyperexcited by my discovery that I had to stop reading.

14 June

Reading now carefully—and for the first time in its entirety—Jung's *Psychologie und Alchemie,* and reading especially his *Psychologie des Übertragung,* I am astonished by the coincidence of our interpretations: often Jung uses expressions almost identical with my own (particularly in *Psychologie des Übertragung*). However, I published *Alchemia asiatică* in 1935, and the essence of that little book was found already in my *Cuvântul* columns of 1932–33—hence ten or twelve years before Jung.

18 June

For two days, a continuous torrential, tropical rain. Impossible to take a few steps, even in the garden. The novel goes forward—rather slowly, but I'm satisfied.

25 June

Steady rain. I have interrupted the novel and have begun work on the article for *La Nouvelle revue française:* "Les mythes du monde moderne." Jean Paulhan wrote me two more letters insisting that I send it to him as soon as possible.

BASEL, *30 June*

I see Karl Meuli at the university. He tells me that he has just been speaking about my interpretation of the symbolism of *renovatio* in *Le Mythe de l'éternel retour;* he applied this interpretation to the Greek Thesmophories. I don't know why, but this detail gives me unusual pleasure. Maybe it's because, while writing my book, I never thought of the Greek rituals, just as I didn't think of a great many other things. And yet my observations are verified everywhere, which means that they have the value of a "system," that I've succeeded in delineating general structures of religious thought.

15 July

At Henri-Charles Puech's. He describes Jean Baruzi's death: he let himself die of starvation. Extraordinary particulars about him and his brother. Jean's amazing timidity. Once, when he was just an assistant at the Collège de France, he saw on a posted list of courses the word "Professor" in front of his name. Immediately he wrote a considerable number of memos to all the professors of the college, explaining that this monstrosity was not his fault. Then he scratched out the word "Professor" on the announcement and wrote "Assistant" instead. A man passing by saw him and called out from behind him indignantly: "*Jaloux!*"

27 July

At Gallimard I meet Jean Paulhan. He is surprised to find me "so young"; he imagined me much older and bearded. Just now he's reading *Traité,* but he has read the article in *Diogène* ("La Nostalgie du paradis") and is delighted with it. He puts questions to me one after another, without giving me time to answer at length, as I'd like. He finds "extraordinary" all that I've observed about shamanism; he is excited about the secret shamanic languages. He gives me *La Preuve par l'étymologie.*

ASCONA, *20 August*

This morning I present my lecture. I hadn't succeeded in writing the last pages and had to improvise.

* * *

Tucci tells me that Dasgupta died in February at Allahabad. He had been named professor at the University of Allahabad. He had scarcely had time to hold classes for three weeks.

Thus closes a chapter in my life, begun on an afternoon in December 1928 in the library of the Theosophical Society at Adyar, when I met Dasgupta for the first time. (I had written to him five or six months earlier, and he had assured me that I could come to Calcutta and work with him. However, I was not expecting to meet him at Adyar. He was there on account of the manuscripts of the Theosophical Society.)

22 August

A visit to the Rieder Museum in Marcote, near Lugano, to see the "famous collection" of Romanian icons and art objects. A complete disappointment. Except for the villa and garden of the museum, nothing of beauty, not even a single icon. I am with a whole group of friends and acquaintances, and I almost apologize to them; I tell them that the bad taste of the Swiss collector made him make an invariably inferior selection. The house is full of flowers arranged in funereal fashion. Sometimes they almost suffocate me; I feel as though I'm in a room with a corpse. The owner has a strange manner. In the basement a "boyar" dining room—atrocious! Full of flowers. I am told that the owner eats alone, with his shades and his memories.

GENEVA, *2 September*

We arrived here tonight, rather tired. Hôtel Richemond. At 5:00 P.M. "porto de bienvenue" in la Cour St. Pierre. I meet again members of the Società di Europea di Cultura: Babel, Ungaretti, Monteverdi, Campagnuolo, Carnera, and the old faithfuls Jean Wahl, Jean Amrouche, and Jean Lescure. I find Delfim Santos unchanged after nine years. I meet Julian Marias, about whom Ortega spoke to me so enthusiastically ten years ago. Marias tells me that he has written a book about Ortega and that a second, a response to three Jesuits, is in the press.

5 September

I gave the lecture yesterday.* Many people; a success. My audacity in daring to judge the European crisis through the eyes of others, of non-Europeans, and therefore to judge it in a *religious perspective*—surprised and pleased. Aimé Patri told me at Ascona that this text is too important to remain buried in the collective volume of *Rencontres internationales,* published by Baconniere. He proposed that I modify it and publish it in a Parisian review.

After the lecture, Jean Chauvel, French ambassador at Berne, invites us, together with the Gafencos, to his place. At Bergues, in the apartment once occupied by Titulescu, the ambassador speaks to me about Guénon; the consul-general talks about India. We leave then by car for the Gafencos's villa outside the city, on the shore of the lake.

* * *

Those ladies who inevitably gather around after every lecture and talk to me about India, yoga, "liberation."

PARIS, *9 October*

Last evening I walked along rue St. Jacques en route to Hunwald's place. An autumnal fog and an empty street in front of

---

*"Religious Symbolism and Modern Man's Anxiety," published as chapter 9 of *Myths, Dreams and Mysteries*—TRANS.

me—the solitude and silence one finds so abruptly in Paris just a few steps after emerging from a youthful throng, such as I had encountered on rue St. Michel between Dupont and Luxembourg only a few minutes earlier. A fog, and the veiled lights of the street lamps. From a bistro came the strains of a love song, an almost old-fashioned one, which the radio station had just then revived. Several young people at the bar, seeming out of place there because they appeared to be students whereas the bar belonged to another decade. And then I saw, crossing the street ahead of me, a young woman with a short jacket over her shoulders and wearing black slacks; I watched her as she entered the bistro to purchase cigarettes. For a few minutes I had the impression of being at a cinema house, discovering suddenly that the film had been made in a familiar setting, in my Paris of seven or eight years ago—and all at once an incomprehensible bliss engulfed me. I regained another time. If I live that long, I'll be able to be happy twenty or thirty years from now remembering a walk like this one, in Bois de Boulogne, alone, toward sunset—walks which I, in my infinite naïveté, think that I forget, *that they don't engage me with anything.*

10 November

Now and then an enthusiasm for Dacia and Zalmoxis "seizes" me. I return then to Herodotus's text, which I've read and reread twenty or thirty times before, and to the other little testimonies to the beliefs of the Getae, collected in the notebooks of 1941–42 at Lisbon. For several days, I'm like one possessed; I do nothing but read them over, dream in the margins of the documents, and write many pages with observations, comments, and plans for studies and further research. Then, as usual, the whole thing subsides one morning and I return to my interrupted schedule of work.

Undated, 1953

I don't know why, but I recalled this detail: a year ago, T.B. found me at my work table, with a Sanskrit text open before me. It was Nāgārjuna's *Mūlamadhyakakārikās,* and I couldn't refrain from speaking to him about the grandeur, profundity, and originality of

Nāgārjuna's thought, saying, among other things, how much I regretted
that these "Fundamentals of the Middle Way" had not been translated*
so that they might be available to Western philosophers and logicians (I
was thinking especially of Stephane Lupasco). After listening to me and
looking once again at the books on my desk, T.B. said: "If you only
knew how much I admire you—spending your time with such boring
things! How can anyone *today* still be interested in what the Indians,
Chinese, Annamese, and others like them have thought?"

It would have been futile to argue. But I was reminded then of an
autumn afternoon in 1945 when I was working on *Techniques du Yoga*
on rue des Saints-Pères. Cioran had come to see me, and his eyes fell
on the *Vijñaptimātrasiddhi* by Hiuan-tsang, in La Vallée-Poussin's
translation. He began to leaf through it, excited. "How fortunate you
were to encounter Indian thought at twenty!" he exclaimed. "Only
texts like these are worth reading. How could one read anything else
today, after having read Hegel, Husserl, and Sartre? Could you still read
Leibniz? Or some 'modern thinker' such as E. Boutroux? How
boring!"

PARIS, *June 1954*

We've returned to rue de la Tour, but we no longer recognize
the place. All the furniture, rugs, drapes, etc. have been transported
to the sixth floor where Delia and René Laforgue have recently
moved. We have a bed, a few chairs—and I a small table for writing,
at which I work, hunching over. I remember suddenly the last weeks
spent at Cascaes, in a half-ruined building (a town hall in the process
of being torn down) on Praça de Pescados, with Călin Botez's little
boy crawling around on the floor, frowning, fighting off flies, picking
up the debris which the men working outside brought us. I'd like to
reread my journal from that time, but all my papers and books are
still at the place on rue Duhesme. I brought only the manuscript of
the novel with me here.

---

*The *Mūlamadhyakakārikās* was recently translated and discussed in a commentary by
a student of mine at the University of Chicago, Frederick J. Streng [author's note, 1971].

Guillermou has finished translating the first part, and Christinel works at the typewriter day and night in the back room. It frightens us both, how large the novel is turning out to be. Who will read it? Who will buy it?

* * *

I promised Brice Parain I'd leave him a typed copy of part 1 before going away on vacation.

I've resumed work on chapter 6, the penultimate one. Am struggling with a mysterious sadness and a great, deep weariness. I keep telling myself that I ought to take a rest, because I'm not as young as I used to be, but I feel that it's too late, that whatever may happen I no longer have time, that the only thing I still desire is to be delivered from this novel—and after that, let come what may.

* * *

With a great effort, Chrtistinel last night finished typing the last chapter of the translation of part 1, and this morning I went to Gallimard and left the manuscript for Brice Parain.

Tomorrow morning we leave for Ascona.

18 June

Those paintings on the walls of paleolithic caves, with bisons, bears, wounded gazelles brought down by spears or arrows. It is a matter of magic—but in what sense? The effect was not on the *game* but on the *hunter.* Compare with the effect produced, during the Occupation in Paris by a dagger piercing a swastika.

Karma is also a kind of "history": man is the result of his own past freedoms; he is conditioned, that is, by those freedoms.

20 June

In oriental spirituality, the Occident meets again "Platonism," archetypes, exemplary models.

ASCONA, 26 June

Five years ago, when I began to write *Noaptea de Sânziene,* I knew almost nothing except the ending. I knew that after twelve years Ştefan would meet Ileana again in a forest and that he would recognize the automobile which (as it had seemed to him) had disappeared or ought to have disappeared in the forest Băneasa on the Night of St. John, 1936. Those twelve years constituted in my mind a perfect cycle, closed and homologous to cosmic cycles (the Great Year, etc.). The reunion in 1948 was to redeem all their trials and sufferings. Until very recently, even after I'd begun writing the final chapter and was approaching the reunion in the forest at Royaumont, I believed that the reunion would mean, for both, the beginning of a "New Life" (*renovatio*). Ştefan's "search" I had homologized to an initiatory Quest. The refinding of Ileana was equivalent to initiatory fulfilment (the victorious facing of all the initiatory "ordeals and trials"). Now, today, I have realized that it is a matter of something else: Ştefan was obsessed by "the car that was to have disappeared at midnight," the car in which Ileana "was to have come" to Băneasa in 1936. What seems so strange in the meeting at Băneasa, stranger than his incomprehensible love for Ileana (incomprehensible because he continues to be in love with Ioana) is his obsession with her car. Now, everything is explained if Ileana's car—real at Royaumont twelve years later—is the cradle of their death. Ileana, as it seems to me now, no longer loves him. Ştefan's Quest, therefore, was a quest for death. Ileana shows herself to be that which she was from the beginning: an angel of Death (except that, in the beginning, without the *real car,* her true destiny could not be perceptible). Autos have, in the novel, an archetypal function, and the forewarned reader will soon observe that whenever the image of a car appears a "rupture of plane" occurs and destinies are decided or become perceptible. The symbolism of Death *imposes itself on me* as I write the last chapter. I don't know yet whether they will both die in an accident on that night—although this conclusion would be the only plausible one. Ştefan has "solved all the mysteries" (d-na Zissu, Partenie, etc.); on the anecdotal plane this "understanding" corresponds to the "final understanding" of the sage, which is at the same time his tombstone (in a sense, life holds no more surprises for him; he is a "living dead man"). Ştefan's historical existence would no longer have any meaning without Ileana, once he has succeeded in finding her again. And if it seems to him that Ileana no longer loves him, then there's nothing more left for him to do in this world.

But it could be that at the last moment another solution will impose itself on me—what, I don't know. Because the symbolism of Death permits of *everything:* an extinction or a regeneration, a true *incipit vita nova*. We shall see.

7 July

Today, at 11:35 A.M., I finished writing and transcribing the last page. The novel is ended.

In the last few days I wrote while struggling not only with sadness but also with an almost physical oppression. It was quite impossible for me to resist the destiny which had been decided long ago and without my knowledge: that Ştefan and Ileana would perish on that Night of St. John, 1948, somewhere on a road leading to Lausanne. I wrote in a state of constant tension—and it was as though the weather outside reflected my inner storm, because all the time there were lightning flashes and gales, which were followed by a cold, hard, autumn-like rain. So far I'm unable to enjoy the fact that I've concluded that book.

* * *

Toward evening, Christinel and I walk to Ascona, to a café near Pancaldi.

9 July

Yesterday and today, the strange state of sadness, fatigue, and despair has continued. People you've carried around with you for five years, to whom you gave breath and whom you nourished from your own being. . . . An emptiness inside. I find myself somehow without a meaning in life, exhausted.

We go to Locarno so I can cash a check. I leave my passport at the bank and don't discover that it is missing until evening. This is the first time in my life that I've forgotten my passport and left it somewhere— that is, lost my "identity." It would be interesting to know how a psychologist would interpret this. Perhaps the presentiment that I have left behind an "identity," that "something" has died in me or for me? That I want to escape from something, to free myself from a past I no longer acknowledge as mine?

14 July

I must write someday a long study on the "origins" of philosophy—show, that is, the passage from cognition through myths and symbols (as practiced in archaic worlds) to systematic philosophy. Examples: (1) that which is "archaic" in Plato (for instance, the prehistory of the theory of Ideas: from the *exemplary image* to the Platonic *Idea*); (2) initiation is equivalent to philosophy. Initiation represents "death" to the plane of profane experience and "resurrection" to religious experience—that is, access to metaphysical knowledge. I must emphasize the obstetric symbolism attested in both initiatory rituals and Socratic maieutics.

For Husserl, phenomenology entails the abolition of profane experience, of the "natural man." That which phenomenologists call the "natural attitude" is the profane state, the preinitiatory condition. Just as access to the real is obtained by means of phenomenological reduction, so also by means of initiation one penetrates into the sacred plane; that is, the spirit gains access to the absolute (= the real).

August

Ponder this particular: that man, although made from earth, is derived nevertheless from the sun. The earth detached itself from the sun before man appeared, and this act became in a sense the exemplary model for all human "falls" and "coolings."

What I've written is clumsy and obscure, but when I have time someday I'll explain at length what I mean.

August

I'd like someday to write a "prehistory" of all the parareligious customs that still survive in modern societies. Father Christmas or St. Nicholas who is supposed to descend the chimney and appear suddenly, *unexpectedly,* in the room. The chimney which appears that way in the unforgettable Yiddish play "The Singer of His Sorrows" (as a lycée pupil, I saw it in Bucharest, presented by a troupe from Vilna). Now, age-old beliefs show us that the god or his messenger (the "ancestor," the dead) descends and disappears through the chimney of the house. The chimney was a kind of "road" between two worlds. As Coomaraswamy wrote: "The chimney, at the same time *caminus* and passageway, through which Agni begins his journey and we ourselves must ascend toward heaven. . . ." The chimney, the hearth equals *axis mundi:* rupture of plane, therefore possibility of communication between Heaven, Earth, and Hell. What is so fascinating is that this archaic image is still preserved in the soul of the modern, desacralized man.

November

All of a sudden I recall Kafka's *Metamorphosis,* and I think about the fact that in the beliefs of a great many peoples men, on dying, are transformed into animals. Of course, Kafka wasn't thinking of death but rather of a zoological regression, a "fall" onto inferior planes of organic life. This diminution, homologous with larval existences, belongs undoubtedly to Kafka's terrors and nightmares. But it is interesting to notice that death as such is considered on a folkloric (therefore religious) plane as being the regression into a larval existence, a diminution of an ontological nature. It might be, therefore, that a vision so "modern" as that of Kafka rediscovers a very ancient fear of death, buried somewhere in the unconscious.

8 December

Le Yoga: immortalité et liberté has appeared. I haven't had time to rejoice; I'm working furiously on *Forgerons et alchimistes.* I hope I can finish it before Christmas. Am trying to say more in this book than I've dared to say previously in my other scientific books.

January 1955

From Simone Weil: "Nous sommes retournés. Nous naissons tels. Rétablir l'ordre, c'est défaire en nous la créature" [We are returners. We are born such. To reestablish order is to annul the creature in us]. This means "faire passer du créé dans l'incréé" [to pass from the created into the uncreated]. I'm astonished to find in an authentically modern religious experience an archaic pattern: the reintegration of the superabundant primordial, the only true reality.

11 January

The Greek temple was called *naos, néôs*—that is, "ship." Ponder this image: the Temple, that is, sacrality expressed in bulk, is conceived as a boat. Thanks to which one can travel (of course, *toward* Heaven, *through* Heaven), one can cross the waters (= nonbeing, darkness, chaos, etc.). The idea that the perfect passage can be made only in a "vessel," that is, in an "enclosed form" which protects one from disintegration, dissipation, dissolution (= dissolving into Water).

21 February

Last night I am suddenly awakened by a terrible, sinister odor coming from a mole in my right armpit. I go to the bathroom to look at it: bloody, mixed with a very thin pus, slightly sticky. I wash it as well as I can and try to go back to sleep. Impossible. Two hours of insomnia, terrorized by black thoughts. I fall asleep, I believe, rather late, after I hear the first trains going to Paris.

It's strange—it seems to me that I've thought a great deal about death. But what kind of death? A sudden, instantaneous passage into the beyond. A day or two of recollection, meditation, perhaps also some physical suffering to detach me more quickly from earth—and then the passage. I've never thought about a *slow* death of this kind (although, oddly enough, I've prayed constantly not to be fated to have cancer, to die the *other way*). At first, kept in that terrible presence of death by my corpse-like effluvias, it was impossible for me to think about the soul, about postexistence, about the serene detachment from the body. Plato, India, initiation through death and rebirth—all these were far from me. Present only was the corpse. I sensed its presence with an extraordinary acuteness and plenitude, as though there were nothing else in death but it. And yet I knew that wasn't so. With an effort of will, I succeeded sometimes in separating myself from my dead body and in thinking about *death*.

And then, another kind of fear came over me. How unready I am to pass beyond! A feeling of guilt: almost nothing of that which I *had* to do have I done. The "messages" which only now am I prepared to transmit: my religious and philosophical books, perhaps also literary works. I've been playing the program of a life of about sixty years, and lo, at less than forty-eight I have already in my nostrils the stench of my own corpse! To be sure, I told myself, there will be an operation, I'll be cared for, and so on—but that will give me only a year, at most two; with my strength ebbing away little by little, I'll be incapable of writing another real book. I'll have to be satisfied, at best, with articles and the *Journal*.

But all these thoughts and calculations were nothing. Present only was the odor of the corpse. I imagined myself with my right arm amputated, I saw myself writing with my left hand, greeting people with the left hand lifted. In vain. This image of the "casting off" of that part of my body which had begun to rot didn't calm me. And all at once I thought about that book I'm preparing to write, *Mort et initiation*. Up to now, I've seen it "from outside," as a work of erudition and philosophy. I've been wrong; I haven't understood the essential thing. Death is an initiation, and any death, intelligently assumed, can be equated with an initiation. But "symbolic death" (ritual, initiatory death) is not only suffering, torment, sickness, etc.; is is also the experience of your own corpse, the reconciliation with that simple fact which we forget: that we are not only *in passage* but also in a state of decomposition, and we must *accept* this cadaver which is our flesh, we must reconcile ourselves to the idea that *we are this also:* a corpse. We must not think only of the soul. That would be too simple. In my case, it didn't work at all: it didn't calm me in the least to think that I was going to be separated from by body. I became reconciled only by accepting myself as I was, assuming my own corpse-like odor, telling myself that this belongs to me. Perhaps only so valorized could my fear of last night be integrated: I sensed in it the initiatory terror. I said to myself, I must pass through all these things in order to be able to live again, another way, in another place.

ROME, *25 April*

The Congress for the History of Religions. Joachim Wach tells me that he has invited me to present the Haskell Lectures at the

University of Chicago . . . next year. This year, Heiler will be the lecturer. I don't have too much hope of being able to go to Chicago. An American visa seems inaccessible.

TASCH, *August*

I'm writing in this notebook less and less frequently. I don't understand very well why—but I *sense* the reason.

We came to this hamlet at 1,700 meters a week ago. Magnificent weather. Bracing walks—but, above all, literary intoxication. At Casa Gabriella during July I wrote the novella *Fata căpitanului* (The Captain's Daughter). Here I have begun a long narrative, *Pe strada Mântuleasa* (On Mântuleasa Street [published in English as *The Old Man and the Bureaucrats*]), which excites me very much. I'm writing as many as eight or nine pages a day, as I did in youth. I'm sinking little by little into a Bucharestian mythology that has lain dormant for fifteen years.

In June, Guillermou hastily corrected the proofs of *Forêt interdite* (the definitive title of the novel). The book will appear in the fall. I know that my literary fate in the West depends on this novel—but I can't do anything, can't intercede either with friendly critics or with Gallimard (for publicity, etc.). The only thing that matters to me at the moment is to finish the novella.

Enrico Grassi, whom I met in Rome, is asking me insistently for a small volume for the series he is editing, *Rowohlt Deutsche Enzyklopädie*. The first numbers will appear in the fall. Grassi wants me to write *Das Heilige und das Profane*. Rowohlt has sent the contract to me here. One hundred sixty typed pages by January. I don't know what I'll do. I have to finish several studies and complete the little book promised to Carlo Diano (*Centre du monde, temple, maison*). And this summer (the first, since 1950, without Eranos), I'm saving for literature only!

Index